A Partnership for Good?

Scottish Politics and the Union Since 1880

For Evan Charles Stewart

A PARTNERSHIP FOR GOOD?

Scottish Politics and the Union Since 1880

RICHARD J. FINLAY

JOHN DONALD PUBLISHERS LTD
EDINBURGH

ISBN 0 85976 411 7

British Library Cataloguing in Publication Data
A catalogue record for this book is available from the
British Library.

Printed and bound by Bell & Bain Ltd, Glasgow

Acknowledgements

Firstly, I would like to thank Donald Morrison and Russell Walker of John Donald Publishers Limited for their saintly patience in waiting for this book to arrive. My colleagues at the Research Centre in Scottish History at the University of Strathclyde have been supportive beyond the call of duty. Professor Tom Devine has been a pillar of strength and a source of great encouragement. Dr John Young has helped with his sense of humour and I have benefited considerably from our discussions on Scottish history. Michael Fry has listened to many of the ideas in the book with a sympathetic and critical ear and has been most generous with his advice. Margaret Hastie has helped to deflect many of the distractions which can hold up the writing of a book. Innes Kennedy, Graham Wynn, David Forsyth, Catriona Macdonald and Anne Baker have helped sharpen up my ideas.

My colleagues in the Department of History at Strathclyde have been equally supportive. Special thanks go to Professor James McMillan, Professor Hamish Fraser, Professor Tom Tomlinson and Dr Simon Adams. I am especially grateful to Dr Conan Fischer for sharing his wisdom and knowledge on nationalism and national identity. Thanks go out to my colleagues in the Politics Department. Dr James Mitchell, as ever, has been generous with his expertise on Scottish politics. I have benefited from discussions with Professor Arthur Midwinter on the changing nature of the Union.

Professor Ted Cowan has provoked, cajoled, insulted and encouraged my understanding of Scottish history. Thanks to his exertions, I have tried to write in a more accessible style. Thanks to Lizanne Henderson for putting up with us.

Jack Finlay and Edd Brown have put up with more than most in the completion of this book. My heartfelt thanks to both of them. Others on the roll call are: Eleanor Finlay, Eddy Crossley, Kate and John Esplin, Colin Finlay, Seonaid Finlay, Katie Jane,

Hannah and Nikkita, Brenda Kemp, Ethel Ackroyd, Greta Stewart, the late and great Duncan Stewart and Fiona Wynn.

Thanks to Iain Martin for his friendship and our long discussions on politics, life and the universe. I have received some of my best advice from Alastair Stewart. Thanks to May Stewart for putting up with me every Thursday night when I invaded her home. Thanks, with dedication, to Evan Stewart. More than anyone, he has had to put up with my inane ramblings. I hope this book does justice to our friendship: (I can just see Ted Cowan reading this and thinking 'that wouldn't be hard').

Glasgow, 1997   RJF

Contents

Abbreviations

H.C. Debs.	*House of Commons Debates*
ILP	Independent Labour Party
NLS	National Library of Scotland
SHRA	Scottish Home Rule Association
SNC	Scottish National Convention
SNL	Scottish National League
SNP	Scottish National Party
STUC	Scottish Trade Union Congress

INTRODUCTION
Scottish Politics, National Identity and the Union

The title of this book has been shamelessly stolen from the Conservative government's publication *Scotland and the Union: A Partnership for Good* which was produced as a result of John Major's 1993 *Taking Stock* exercise regarding the efficacy of existing constitutional arrangement between Scotland and the rest of the United Kingdom. The report set its face against any change to the *status quo* and made no concessions to the apparent public clamour for political devolution. The title of the document neatly encapsulated the essence of Conservative opinion; the Union was for good in that it benefited Scotland and it was also for good in the sense that the Union would, and should, last forever. In the last hundred years or so, most Scots would have agreed with these two propositions. However, for almost the last three decades, an increasing number of Scots have begun to question those most fundamental tenets of Scottish Unionism. The object of this book is to examine changing perceptions of the Union in Scottish political life since the late nineteenth century.

The Union of Scotland and England has been of fundamental importance in shaping Scottish historical development since its formal political inception in 1707. It has also been a crucial benchmark in defining Scottish and British national identities in Scotland, and the often complex relationships which have arisen between them. [1] Recently, Scottish national identity has become the focus of much scholarly attention largely because Scottish political behaviour has diverged from the rest of the United Kingdom in that the Scots have repeatedly rejected the Conservative Party at the polls. Although support for the Scottish National Party (SNP) has risen, it still has some way to go before it can realise its aim of securing an electoral mandate for independence. Nonetheless, the critical difference between Scotland and England, in a political sense, has been the decline of Conservative fortunes north of the border and many commentators have ascribed this to a form of Scottish nationalist sentiment, with the emphasis on nationalist with a small 'n'. Over the last decade, most Scots voters have perceived the Conservative Party as representing the political interests of southern England, rather than those of the United Kingdom as a whole. Furthermore, the Thatcher ethos attacked mainstream Scottish political values concerning the role of the state and Scotland has been subjected to a barrage of unpopular legislation, all of which has caused Conservative Party support in Scotland to plumet to unprecedented depths. Unlike all the other oppostion parties, the Conservative Party has been unique in its opposition to the creation of a Scottish parliament, which has had the effect of associating the Union of Scotland and England in the mind of most of the electorate with the unpopular policies of the Conservative governments since 1979. More than anything, it has been the experience of unpopular British government which has fuelled the demand for a Scottish parliament, either working within or without the constitutional framework of the United Kingdom. This has become an established facet of Scottish politics and debates about the future of the Union are never far from the top of the Scottish political agenda. All of which has helped to give Scottish politics a heightened sense of a distinctive national dimension.[2] If the opinion polls are anything to go by, it seems as if the overwhelming majority of Scots want to change the constitutional relationship between England and Scotland which has lasted for nearly three hundred years. Although much work has been done by sociologists and political scientists on the peculiarities of Scotland as a stateless nation, and the reasons why the Scots are expressing increasing unease with the Union, historians have had little to say on the matter, nor have they offered a historical explanation as to how the present state of affairs has come to exist.[3] At this point, it is perhaps an opportune moment to say something about the historian's approach to the nature of Scottish political relations with the British state since the late nineteenth century. Historians have written extensively about Scottish nationalism, indeed over-written, according to one eminent historian, and in spite of their lack of prominence in Scottish political developments over the last century, we know more about the nationalists than other, arguably more important, political parties and movements.[4] In part, the answer to this historical imbalance lies with the fact that most work on Scottish nationalism was written in response to the rise of the SNP in the late nineteen sixties and seventies and historians were suddenly posed the question why Scottish nationalism should have emerged at that particular point in time. For many it seemed strange that Scottish nationalism, which to all intents and purposes had not risen its head since the eighteenth century, should suddenly emerge at a time when nationalism was perceived as romantic and backward looking. Trends in the world at large seemed to point towards internationalisation and homogenisation; the world was supposed to be getting smaller and more similar. Britain was claimed to be the most homogenous industrial society in the world and if anything, the differences between Scotland and England should have been disappearing into a uniform Britishness.[5] Such values and assumptions affected the historical writing of the time. British national identity was assumed to be natural and taken for granted, while Scottish nationalism was seen as an exotic deviation from the norm which had somehow survived the onslaught of British assimilation. However, the current political climate calls such assumptions into question as Scottish national identity, rather than British national identity, is much more clearly identified as a major political force in Scotland. Such changes in the Scottish political climate have necessitated a historical re-evaluation of our dominant values and assumptions. Britishness in Scotland is something which can no longer be taken for granted as a natural development and it is the aim of this book to chart how a modern British political identity developed north of the border and how this co-existed with a Scottish national identity.

A further problem with much of the existing literature is a tendency to see Scottish nationalism and the threat to the Union as a peculiar phenomenon of the late post-war era. In fact, this is not the case. As will be shown, Scottish politicians since the late nineteenth century have consistently debated the question of constitutional realignment and have striven to modernise and adapt the Union in response to new circumstances and demands. Furthermore, the attitudes of politicians to the Union have gone through fundamental changes in this period. Debates about the Union and the place of Scotland's relationship to the rest of the United Kingdom have been an important facet of Scottish politics and it has a long and fascinating pedigree. By taking a historical approach to the issue of Scottish political attitudes to the Union it will be possible to show how the British state has been remarkably successful in accommodating Scottish political aspirations and also, it will show that there has been a great deal of fluidity in the debate. The book will point out that many of the current issues regarding Scottish home rule have already been aired in the past. The 'West Lothian Question' was first raised in the 1880s, for example. If nothing else, this book might help to put the on going debate about Scotland's constitutional future within its proper historical context.

As is well known, history tends to favour the winners. Most historical writing is dictated by the demands of contemporary society which tends to reflect its own interests back into the past. Environmental history and the history of women, for example, are areas of important study because today's society regards them as important and consequently, we want to know about them in the past. To a Victorian historian, the study of women and the environment would have seemed bizarre because such subjects were not considered important or meaningful by Victorian society. Our preoccupation with historical winners raises problems for the study of Scottish politics and the Union because as yet, no clear winners in the constitutional debate have emerged. History works at its best when there are clear lines of demarcation. For example, had the SNP obtained an electoral mandate in the elections of 1974 and brought about independence, historians would have busily set about showing how this was done. The ancestors of the SNP in the 1850s, the National Association for the Vindication of Scottish Rights, would have been the subject for endless PhD theses and almost certainly, they would have been exhalted for their foresight and wisdom. A nationalist victory will enhance the historical significance of all past nationalist organisations, just as a devolutionist or status quo victory will enhance the historical reputations of previous proponents of these schemes. Historians are cautious creatures who take their cue as to what is important in the past from what is important in the present, and the current uncertainty about Scotland's political future makes the task of writing about the Union all the more difficult. After all, if the Scots decide to stick with the unreformed Union and interest in home rule and independence died away, then this book will only be of marginal interest to Scottish society and would find itself quickly consigned to the bargain basement.

Given such problems and the conceptual difficulties associated with the stateless nation, it is no surprise that most of the scholarly work in recent times which has dealt with Scottish national identity and its political relationship with the Union has come from the stable of sociologists and political scientists. Such work has been valuable in providing theoretical frameworks, international comparisons and it has generated much discussion as to the peculiarities of Scottish historical development. However, from the historian's perspective, such work is marred by a number of weakness. Firstly, given the nature of such studies, a premium is placed on conceptualisation and theory which endeavours to provide an all-embracing model of Scottish development. The emphasis is on the big picture and detailed microscopic analysis is sacrificed in favour of generalisations and sweeping statements which often are not backed up with hard historical evidence or facts. Secondly, a lot of the complexities and detail have to be glossed over in order to fit a theoretical package. While this may be justifiable in some academic disciplines, it is quite unacceptable to the historian. Thirdly, much of the recent work written from a sociological perspective has been based on interpretations of secondary sources and has not been based on original research of the primary sources. Yet, it is only through an examination of contemporary records that we can build up a picture as to how contemporaries perceived their national identity and its relationship to the Union. Finally, given the complexities of social and political theory, much of the language used in such studies is of a very specialised nature and is often inaccessible to the general reader. The advantage of a historical approach is that it is under no obligations to fit into any theoretical moulds. Ragged edges and untidy corners do not matter. The primary objective is to explain why things happened as they did at a particular point in time and this has to be based on historical evidence.

This book is an attempt to redress these deficiencies and examine how the Scots have perceived the Union over the last hundred years or so and how this has affected the evolution of Scottish national identity and, in turn, how this has manifested itself in British political developments. All too often, there is a tendency among politicians and commentators of our own time to throw back into the past their present ideas of the Union, rather than see it as an organic development which has been changed and adapted over time to suit new conditions and circumstances. Indeed, it is only by looking at how Scots have perceived the role and function of the Union in the past that the historian can chart how the Scots thought of themselves as being both Scottish and British and how the two were melded together. However, perhaps of greater importance is the changing relationship between Scottishness and Britishness and the different emphasis which was placed upon them by different Scots at different times that gives us our real clues as to the evolution of national identity in Scotland during this period. Furthermore, it is a time when mass democracy was allowing more Scots an input into the political process, and consequently, the opportunity to express their national identity through the ballot box. In this way, it is possible to talk about a genuine national identity, in the sense that for most of the period under review a significant element of the nation was politically franchised, and thus had a say in the nation's political development. This has to be borne in mind because it is too easy to look at the ideas of the elite and pass them off as those of the people.[6] It is the tensions which often arose from competing visions of Scottishness, Britishness and the Union that forms the core of the book's analysis.

Given the object of this study, it goes without saying that much time will be spent discussing national identity, or at least its political manifestations. However, Scottish national identity poses a number of problems for the historian which can be defined in four broad categories. They are; the highly individual nature of national identity which often encompasses many layers or sub-identities; the difficulty of quantifying and measuring national identity; the relationship of national identity to politics and culture; and finally, finding a definition of Scottish nationalism which can be usefully applied throughout this period. Let us examine each of these in turn.

National identity is a many-layered phenomenon and, as recent distressing examples from around the world show, it is capable of defying rational explanation. Each individual carries his or her own national identity which is unique to that person. It may have similar strands to others in the nation, but at the end of the day, it is the individual who chooses what does or does not make them Scottish. This makes it very difficult to reduce Scottish national identity to a common set of values which all members of the nation share without degenerating into meaningless stereotypes. Furthermore, national identity works in conjunction with other identities, such as class, religion, gender and region and in a great many circumstances, these identities are more likely to determine political action. National identity can be described as the glue which bonds all these other factors into a particular territorial identification, or what the sociologist, Benedict Anderson, calls an 'imagined community'.[7] It is imagined in the sense that everybody in Scotland has a vision of the Scottish nation which they imagine all other Scots identify with. National identity can combine contradictory notions and ideas, and does not lend itself to systematic explanation, hence the issue is often reduced to generalities such as, the Scots are Scottish because they feel themselves to Scottish. While this is very true, we still have the problem that an east coast, Protestant, female, bank manager and a west coast, male, catholic, miner can both believe themselves to be Scottish, but the truth is that their conceptions of Scotland and Scottishness will have very little in common. The first point is that national identity is a fluid and intangible concept which is hard to pin down with any degree of accuracy. If this problem dogs our understanding of Scottish national identity in the present, then it follows that there is no reason to assume that it is any easier to understand in the past.

Our second problem is that national identity does not lend itself to empirical quantification. We can say, for example, how many people voted for the Liberal Party in Scotland in the general election of 1906, but we can not say with any degree of accuracy what percentage of the Scottish electorate in 1906 felt more Scottish than British. By its very nature, nationalism and national identity are composed of intangible qualities and, more often than not, the historian can only detect traces of these. Nationalism tends to be reactive; it emerges in response to a set of particular circumstances such as a perceived threat against the nation or its culture. Most of the time, however, it lies dormant. Take the following example, if three Scots were stranded on a desert island their national identity would not become obvious to them until someone from a different country showed up. The fact that there are few outbursts of direct nationalist sentiment in this period does not mean that the Scots were without a sense of national identity, rather it means that they perceived few direct threats to it. Unlike, say Irish nationalism and national identity, which left clear marks on the historical landscape for historians to chart, Scottish national identity has been more diffuse and circumspect in exposing its nature. To reconstruct Scottish sentiment in the past, the historian has to look at a wide range of sources and carefully filter them for insights into national identity.   Scots have on occasion felt that their identity was under threat and this brought into clear focus how many politicians felt about Scotland, Britain and the Union; hence the book's preoccupation with this key theme. But more often than not, national identity was taken for granted by contemporaries. There was little need to formulate it or give it intellectual expression if it was assumed that everybody knew what it was. Not only are we unable to accurately and empirically measure national sentiment, our key sources into national identity are usually produced at times when there is a perceived threat and therefore tell us more about the crisis facing national identity, rather than national identity itself.

A third difficulty in studying the effect of national identity on Scottish political development is that   nationalism does not always register itself in party political terms. The SNP does not, and never has, monopolised political nationalism, and other political parties have frequently played the Scottish card for their own ends. A key element in Unionist thought was that loyalty to the Union did not contravene a deep and patriotic commitment to Scottish nationality. As will be seen, the notion of the Union as a partnership between Scotland and England was central to Scottish political thought in this period and for many it was a partnership of two equal countries. The Union in no way implied subservience for many Scots. Also, many Scots have, and continue to, express their national identity in a non political way, be that on the football terraces or in the art galleries. Even when nationalism does manifest itself within the political arena, it is often on a non-party basis. A too narrow reading of nationalist party fortunes will give only a partial reading into the evolution of the Union. It ignores the ways in which mainstream politicians and parties reacted to the perception of Scottish sentiment. A key element in the development of the government of Scotland has been the ability of the Union to adapt and accommodate nationalist sentiment. More has been changed   by the fear of allowing nationalist discontent to manifest itself in a party political sense than by the presence of a strong nationalist party.

Our final difficulty is one of terminology. Scottish nationalism and national identity have changed over time and it is therefore difficult to define in concrete terms. Scottish nationalism has meant different things to different people at different times. We have to be wary of imposing our own ideas of Scottish nationalism and Unionism back on to the past. For example, home rulers in the 1880s often described themselves as nationalists but did not want to break the Union. Indeed, their argument in favour of a Scottish parliament revolved around the notion that it would strengthen the Union and the British Empire. They would have very little in common with the present day members of the SNP. Likewise, nineteenth century Conservatives would have disagreed with the assimilationist tendencies of the modern British state. Indeed, historically speaking, Conservatives have been in the vanguard of the movement to prevent the encroachment of Scottish local powers from the state. Furthermore, we have to be on our guard against assuming that Scottish nationalism can only take one form. It is all too easy to equate Scottish nationalism as being intrinsically hostile to the British state. This has been a problem with the work of a number of historians who have written about Scottish nationalism because they have, in actual fact, been writing about one particular type of Scottish nationalism. Tom Nairn, for example, has argued that Scottish nationalism failed to develop in the mid-nineteenth century at a time when other European nations began to clamour for political independence. The Scottish bourgeoisie were seduced by the economic benefits of the Union and the nationalism which developed was a stunted and deviant 'tartan monster'. Consequently, Scottish nationalism only begins to emerge as a serious political force from the late 1960s as the problems of the British economy come home to roost and the Scots start to question the economic viability of the Union.[8] However, such a reading of events is based on a very narrow definition of Scottish nationalism. As Christopher Smout has recently argued, Scots in the eighteenth century developed a 'concentric loyalty' which allowed them to compartmentalise their patriotism into Scottish and British components, neither of which was mutually exclusive.[9] Indeed, as will be argued in this book, Scottish nationalism was not only able to exist within the British state and Empire, it was actually extenuated and promoted by the British imperial ethos. The Scots were proud of their achievements as 'Empire Builders' and believed that the British Empire brought out the best of their national characteristics. Nairn and others have made the mistake of assuming that Scottish nationalism must only take one form and that it must work against the British state. However, when we look at the key components of nineteenth century European nationalism, such as racism, imperialism, religious expansionism, economic expansionism, monarchism and militarism, we see the Scots rejoicing in all of those aspects of British imperialism and what is more, they do so as Scots with their own distinctive national characteristics. To claim that Scottish nationalism was deviant in the nineteenth century because it did not follow a particular path is based on hindsight. If we talk about the failure of Scottish nationalism to deliver independence in the nineteenth century then we are guilty of making subjective judgements as to what kind of nationalism is best. Also, we are in danger of preoccupying ourselves with what did not happen and using counter-factual history as the benchmark of our judgements, rather than explaining what did happen which surely ought to be the principal task of the historian. This book has not been written to explain why Scotland did not follow the same historical path as other European nations such as Ireland, rather it is to explain why Scottish political development and national identity have been contained within the Union and why it is that in recent years tensions have emerged which threaten to undermine the existence of the constitutional arrangement between Scotland and England.

NOTES

[1] See D. Broun, R.J. Finlay & M.Lynch (eds), *Image and Identity: The Making and Remaking of Scotland*, (Edinburgh, 1997).
[2] See J.Mitchell, *Strategies for Self-Government: the Campaign for a Scottish Parliament*, (Edinburgh, 1996).
[3] For the work of political scientists and sociologists see Mitchell, *Strategies for Self-Government*, L. Paterson, *The Autonomy of Modern Scotland*, (Edinburgh, 1994) and D. McCrone, *Understanding Scotland: the Sociology of a Stateless Nation*, (London, 1992).
[4] Chris Harvie, *No Gods and Precious Few Heroes*, (London, 1981), p.169.

[5] For a good example of this see J. Blondel, *Voters, Parties, and Leaders: the Social Fabric of British Politics*, (London, 1974), p. 20.

[6] See Linda Colley, *Britons: Forging the Nation, 1707-1837*, (Yale, 1992) and R.J. Finlay, 'North Briton or Caledonia: Scottish Identity in the Eighteenth Century' in Broun, Finlay & Lynch (eds), *Image and Identity*.

[7] B. Anderson, *Imagined Communities: Reflections on the Origins and Spread of Nationalism*, (London, 1983).

[8] T. Nairn, *The Break-Up of Britain*, (London, 1981), p. 162.

[9] T.C. Smout, 'Problems of Nationalism: Identity and Improvement in later Eighteenth Century Scotland' in T.M. Devine (ed), *Improvement and Enlightenment*, (Edinburgh, 1989), pp. 1-22.

CHAPTER ONE
A Nation of Empire Builders: Scotland and the Imperial Partnership in the Victorian Era

The period from 1880 to 1914 was one of profound change in British and Scottish politics. The certainties of the mid-Victorian period were increasingly challenged as the British state had to address significant problems, all of which occupied the thoughts and aspirations of politicians. Fears were mounting as to Britain's position in the world. The Empire appeared to be in danger both from within and without. A spate of enthusiasm for colonial empires had swept Europe and the 'scramble for Africa' was symptomatic of the desire to display and prove national prowess by demonstrating to the world the ability to conquer and control vast tracts of land which were thought to be beyond the pale of civilisation. As the world's foremost colonial power, Britain had most to lose and most to protect in this craze for Empire. Within the white colonial settlements themselves, greater autonomy and the demand for more self-government seemed to be pulling the Empire away from the grip of the mother nations in the British isles. Nearer to home, there was the perennial problem of Ireland which, like a spoiled adopted child, had persistently refused to accept the mantle of imperial responsibility and settle into the family home of the British state. Ireland, it appeared to many politicians at the time, could not shake off the colonial trappings of its birth and in spite of a close association with the benevolent civilisation of the British nation, still chose to behave like some of the 'wilder' elements of the extended British imperial family.

British power was dependent on economic muscle. As the first industrial nation, Britain had a head start on any potential competitors. By the 1880s, Germany and the United States had caught up with and were now surpassing the former champion. While historians looking back at British economic performance in this period have emphasised that the economy was undergoing structural change and, in spite of appearances, still maintained a quite commendable output, many contemporaries perceived such changes as evidence of industrial and economic decline.[1] Indeed, such fears promoted the growth of a productive industry which specialised in prophesying economic doom for the British nation. The political vocabulary of the period 1880-1914 was dominated by phrases which spoke loudly as to underlying fears of British economic vitality. 'Fair Trade', 'Tariff Reform', 'Protectionism', 'Made in Germany' and 'National Efficiency' were the watchwords of those who perceived the decline of British industrial power.[2]

The period also witnessed the prolific outpouring of reports and tracts which exposed the rotten condition of the fabric of British society. Culminating in the shocking state of recruits for the army at the time of the Boer War when eight out of eleven volunteers in Manchester, for example, were deemed unfit for military service, politicians increasingly had to re-evaluate their ideas on the role of government in social policy. Intellectually, the traditional values of laissez faire individualism were giving way to new ideas which emphasised an active role for government in the fields of economic and social policy.[3] In a world of increasing economic and military competition, the survival of Britain and the Empire could not be left to lofty ideals of individual self-help and self-improvement. The working class was emerging as a potential force in the world of politics. After the 1884 Reform Act, they were a clear majority of the electorate and politicians had to take on board their interests, especially as the new ideology of socialism could compete for their affections. Government, which had become increasingly proactive in the field of social policy and social legislation, could only expect this trend to continue.[4]

Politics was dominated by endeavours to resolve these three key issues of imperial government, economic promotion and increased social policy and, if possible, tie them together into one grand scheme. The principal difficulty was, however, that various interest groups attached different degrees of priority to each of the issues. For some clamouring for social policy, the question of imperial government was seen by most as irrelevant, while for others, it was the linchpin.[5] The various sectors of the British economy each had their own priorities and remedies and, more often than not, this would involve the promotion of one sector at the expense of another. It is perhaps to the credit of Joseph Chamberlain that he was able to square the circle. Along with a significant body within the Conservative and Liberal Unionist parties which had been developing momentum from the 1880s, Chamberlain in 1903 advocated a policy of imperial preference and tariff reform which would protect British industry from foreign competition. This, it was argued, would protect and promote British economic interests. The concentration of trade with the Empire would reinforce ties of imperial sentiment and counteract the 'centrifugal forces' which might lead to the break-up of the Empire. Finally, the revenue collected by the government by way of tariffs on imports would be used to fund social policy and social reconstruction.[6]

In its simplest form, the policy had obvious advantages and it attracted a large following in British politics. Yet, it had a great many difficulties. The policy was buffeted by objections from both hostile interest groups and ideological dissenters. It offended the free trade lobby which comprised of traditional working-class voters who feared that tariffs would increase the price of food and harm living standards.[7] Laissez faire Liberals who, whatever their divisions on other aspects of policy, all held faithful to this cannon of liberal faith and argued that free trade was the only way to guarantee British economic competitiveness in the long run. Protectionism, it was claimed, would stultify and hold back economic progress. The favourable aspects of social policy mooted by tariff reform were countered by alternative ways to pay for them. The working-class which might benefit the most from such policies, also bought most food, and if taxes were paid on it, they would end up paying most for social reform. Graduated income tax and land tax appeared to be a more advantageous way of funding social reform as far as the working-class were concerned. Such were the issues which dominated British politics in the period between 1880 and the outbreak of the First World War in 1914, and it was against this backdrop that debates about Scotland and the Union were carried out.

Scotland: A Race of Empire Builders

'Questions of Empire' were of great concern to Scottish politicians in the latter part of the nineteenth century. Indeed, it is only recently that historians have begun to address the role of the Scots in British imperialism and the part this played in the manufacture of Scottish national identity. While much historical attention has often focused on the divisions within Scottish society and its political manifestations, support for the Empire was one of the few issues which commanded a general consensus in Scottish intellectual and political circles.[8] The Scots regarded themselves as a 'mother nation' of the Empire and the Union was portrayed as an imperial partnership with England. The role the Scots played in the creation, maintenance and defence of the British Empire was a source of great pride and they rejoiced in their self-proclaimed status as a 'race of Empire builders'. While imperialism has gone out of intellectual and moral fashion, there has been, perhaps understandably, a marked reluctance to examine this particular aspect of Scotland's recent history. Increasingly, a number of British historians have endeavoured to place the Empire back at the centre of British political history and restore it to its former position of historical importance.[9] As a means of economic regeneration, a symbol of world power and as powerful vehicle of propaganda, the Empire played an important part in the formulation of political policy. Also, historians have begun to examine the complexities of imperialist sentiment and imperial development to illustrate that the Empire was not a monolithic creation.[10] Indeed, it existed in a variety of guises in a variety of stages and the sentiment which accompanied its development was just as varied. British imperial sentiment was composed of various strains from the lofty moralists to the basest jingoists. Furthermore, it has become increasingly apparent that British imperial sentiment contained within it the various nationalisms of the United Kingdom. While many politicians and intellectuals used the terms 'England' and 'Britain' in an undifferentiated fashion, there were important Welsh, Irish and Scottish components of imperial sentiment which laid great stress on their particular national contributions to the British imperial mission.[11]

The Reinvention of Scotland

In order to understand how the British Empire assumed such centrality to Scottish national identity and political development in the nineteenth century it is necessary first of all to examine how the Scots were able to adapt and reinvent themselves in order to accommodate the changed circumstances of the Union in the age of industrialisation.[12] Scottish national identity was thrown into a state of crisis in the early nineteenth century as a result of rapid industrialisation and urbanisation which appeared to be eradicating the distinctive national characteristics of Scottish society. The traditional Scottish institutions of education, law and the Kirk were finding it difficult to adapt to the strains thrown up by the forces of modernisation and industrialisation. The institutions had been the preserve of the 'old' Scottish middle-class and they relied on the power of aristocratic patronage for their positions. In return, the 'old' middle-class acted as intellectual guardians of the status quo. The 'new' middle-class, which was riding high on the success of commercialisation and industrialisation, increasing came to regard patronage as an unacceptable tool of old corruption that denied them their rightful position within society. Before 1832, only one adult male in 125 had the vote, compared with one in eight in England, and the Scottish political system was determined by a mere 4,000 voters.[13] In ecclesiastical life, patronage was a running sore in the Church of Scotland. Evangelicals, drawn mainly from the 'new' middle-class, believed that patronage was used to promote the interests of the landlords at the expense of the spiritual well-being and independence of the Kirk. By the 1820s almost a quarter of Presbyterian adherents had opted out of the Kirk to form their own secessionist churches to escape from patronage and again the 'new' middle-class was at the forefront of this development. In 1832 the middle-class were finally given the vote in the Great Reform Act and a year later there began the start of the 'Ten years Conflict' in the Church of Scotland over the issue of patronage which would eventually culminate in the division of the Kirk in the Disruption of 1843.[14]

The assault on the power of 'old corruption' coincided with the break-down of the parochial system of local government in Scotland. Administered by the Church, the parochial system was designed to cater for the spiritual well-being, education and poor relief of the local parish. Yet, this system was designed for a rural society, and in spite of the best efforts of Thomas Chalmers, the leader of the Evangelicals in the Church of Scotland, it could not be adapted to the new urban conurbations which were sprawling over central Scotland.[15] In 1834, George Lewis published, *Scotland: A Half Educated Nation*, in which he complained that the jewel of the Scottish educational crown, the parochial schools, had fallen into disrepair and many children went uneducated. Ominously, readers were warned that if the system was not repaired crime and disorder would increase.[16] A Royal Commission of 1826 found that the Scottish universities which had attained such intellectual eminence in the eighteenth century Enlightenment were now in a shocking state of disrepair.[17] Young radical Whig lawyers such as Frances Jeffrey and Henry Cockburn looked to England for inspiration and guidance to the future development of the Scottish legal system.[18] Indeed, the more that Scotland could be assimilated to England, the better as the former was more advanced and progressive. The Scottish legal system was associated with backward feudal practices and the 1832 Reform Act was celebrated by Cockburn because it was claimed that it gave Scotland a proper constitution for the first time in its history.[19]

Urbanisation threw up new challenges. The cities were portrayed as citadels of vice in which heathenism, crime, drunkenness and whoredom prospered among the throngs of the destitute who were almost beyond the pale of civilisation. Class tensions manifested themselves in industrial strife in the 1830s and the challenge of Chartism thereafter was ample testament to the increasingly divided nature of Scottish society. The Cholera epidemic of 1832, the Irish famine of 1845 with the resultant widespread immigration of destitute Irish into Scotland and, closer to home, the Highland potato famine of 1846 were cited as evidence of God's wrath and punishment on a wicked and immoral nation. It should come as no surprise to find that contemporaries were very pessimistic as to the prospects for the Scottish nation retaining its distinctive national characteristics. The key institutions were in decline and urbanisation and industrialisation were making the cities and much of the Scottish landscape similar to those in England. Walter Scott moaned that 'what makes Scotland Scotland' was fast disappearing, Henry Cockburn described the process of modernisation as driving out the last vestiges of traditional Scotland and the Rev. James Begg talked about the nation sinking under 'an increasing combination of evils'.[20] It was in this atmosphere of cultural pessimism that the National Association for the Vindication of Scottish Rights was formed in 1853.

Although designed to promote and protect the distinctive national characteristics of Scotland, the Association was not a nationalist movement as we would understand it today. Rather, it was a curious amalgam of disparate interests groups and, in many ways, the Association was similar to other nationalist movements which sprung up in Europe during the mid-nineteenth century in response to the evils of urbanisation and industrialisation. The National Association did not advocate a repeal of the Union. It argued that Scotland had suffered national slights since the Union and that the government of Scotland could be improved by the addition of a Scottish Secretary and some degree of self-government:

> Self government and self administration are not however incompatible with the Union. Scotland will never be improved by being transformed into an inferior imitation of England but by being made a better and truer Scotland.[21]

The movement was a political catch-all which included romantic Tories and radical Liberals; hardly a recipe for success. It campaigned against incorrect heraldic emblems, advocated the building of a monument to Sir William Wallace and lamented the condition of Scotland's historic institutions, particularly the universities. The Association appealed for popular support but little was forthcoming, largely because the grievances upon which the movement seized were almost trivial. As the *Times* acidly put it: 'The more Scotland has striven to be a nation the more she has sunk into a province'[22]. Appeals to the Scottish past did little to rouse public sympathy, largely because few thought Scottish nationality was in danger and, in any case, whatever the problems thrown up by modernity, it was more than compensated by the opportunity to prosper and make money. Furthermore, endeavours to rejuvenate the Scottish institutions found little sympathy among the new middle-class who still regarded them as bastions of aristocratic privilege:

> let us now make one resolute to have Scotland for the Scottish people. Let an association be formed for her protection be formed or all is lost. Let us in this year of 1852 make one gallant stand to revive our nationality, to restore our institutions and

insure to future times our civil rights, our laws and the religion of our fathers.[23]

It was a romantic endeavour to turn back the clock and rejuvenate those institutions which were believed to hold the key to Scottish nationality; the Kirk, the law and education.

Although the National Association received a fair amount of support on a number of issues, it never crystallised into a modern nationalist movement. Most contemporaries saw the Association for what it was and claimed that it was Scotland's very success in the Union which made the nationalist grievances possible. Whatever the attraction of the past, the opportunities of the present were more alluring. If Scotland was being taxed too high then it was because Scotland had become a wealthy nation and the root of this wealth was the Union:

> There is scarcely a house of eminence in commerce or manufactures in the Kingdom which does not to some extent owe its success of Scottish prudence, perseverance and enterprise, there is not an industrial department in which there is not a large infusion of the Scottish element in management.. Within a comparatively short period in the history of a nation, its population has more than trebled. It has led the way in agricultural improvements. Its real property has increased in even greater proportion.[24]

Association fears about emigration were likewise dismissed. Scots were leaving to go overseas and work in the Empire because there were opportunities, not because they were being forced to go. If the Union had problems, they were more than compensated by the benefits: 'Lord Eglington and his co-agitators, admit to the fullest extent that Scotland has largely benefited from the union with the richer country.'[25] No real alarm was raised at the diminishing performance of the old Scottish institutions because at the same time as they were falling into disrepair, new symbols, ideas and values emerged to take their place which offered dynamic opportunities for the expression of Scottish national identity.

The Association failed to break into the mainstream of Scottish politics. The abuse of Scottish heraldry and the flying of the Red Ensign by the Royal Navy were hardly the main concerns of Scottish voters in the 1850s and the outbreak of the Crimean War in 1854 swept away the limited publicity it had received. Yet, the Association for the Vindication of Scottish Rights has received a fair amount of historical attention in recent times. This can be explained by the emergence of Scottish nationalism in the post-war era and a desire by historians to trace the roots of the Scottish National Party. Also, interest has focused on why Scotland failed to develop a modern nationalist movement in the mid-nineteenth century at a time when other European nationalist movements were springing up. According to Tom Nairn, the Scottish bourgeoisie rejected nationalism in favour of the economic benefits offered by the Union with England and the Empire. This, he argues, was instrumental in ensuring that the middle-class support necessary for a successful bourgeois nationalist revolution was absent in Scotland and instead, the Scots were landed with a national identity which was 'stunted and ill formed'; the infamous 'tartan monster'.[26]

Nairn's analysis, however, is driven by the assumption that Scottish nationalism should have developed in the nineteenth century and consequently, much time is spent on discussing what did not happen rather than what did. The terms 'stunted' and 'ill formed' are subjective and driven by contemporary political concerns. This does not do adequate justice to the historical complexities of the evolution of Scottish national identity. The historian should not impose his or her own wish fulfilment on the past, but rather, must endeavour to explain what happened, however unpalatable this may be. Part of the problem can be explained by the fact that Scottish nationalism is assumed to be intrinsically hostile to the British state. In other words, our own contemporary definitions of Scottish nationalism are the only valid ones and anything which does not measure up to this is regarded as deviant. Surely it is incumbent on the historian to explain how Scottish national identity adapted itself to accommodate the British state? As explained earlier in this chapter, the Scottish intelligentsia believed that Scotland was disappearing under a tide of modernity, urbanisation and industrialisation, yet Scottish national identity did not vanish, rather it adapted itself to cope with these new circumstances.

The 'reinvention' of Scotland in the early and mid-nineteenth century comprised three key elements. Firstly, Scotland was located in a mythical past and was increasingly associated with Highland and rural symbolism. Secondly, Scottish cultural values were repackaged to suit laissez faire individualist ideology and the dominant position of the middle-class in Scottish society. Finally, and perhaps most importantly from the perspective of accommodating Scottish national identity to the British state, full use was made of the British Empire as an outlet for the display and promotion of supposed Scottish characteristics.

The spread of rapid urbanisation and industrialisation transformed Scottish society. Scotland in 1850 was markedly different from what it had been in 1750. The period witnessed great endeavours to preserve and fossilise those elements of rural Scotland which were believed to hold the essential characteristics of the Scottish nation. Few would accept the new urban and industrial squalor as the essence of the nation. Walter Scott and others set to work collecting historical manuscripts, folk tales and ballads in order to preserve what they believed to be the relics of a truer and purer Scotland unsullied by modernity. If the distinctiveness of Scotland was being eroded in the present, then an appeal to a distinctive past was one way of maintaining Scotland as a national entity. The cult of Robert Burns was used to remind Scots that their essential national characteristics belonged to a rural and pre-industrial time.[27] Similarly, the Highlands were held in high esteem because it was a landscape unspoiled by modernisation. For many lowland Scots, to journey into the Highlands was to venture into the Scotland of the past. The romaniticisation of Scottish history fulfilled the emotional need for nostalgia in an industrialising society. In 1822, the royal visit of George IV was an occasion of almost tartan hysteria as the leading lights of Scottish society fell over themselves in a bid to present themselves as authentic Highland warriors. The Highlander, with his supposed innate qualities of loyalty and martial prowess were transposed onto the Scots in general. It is perhaps one of the greatest paradoxes of Scottish history that at a time when the Highlands were being cleared, the symbols of a people which had be despised as uncivilised and barbaric in the eighteenth century were now being appropriated for the Scottish nation as a whole.[28]

The novels of Walter Scott demonstrated the heroic qualities of the Scot in a semi mythical past. Furthermore, they gave ideological credence to the Union in which the Scots had now found their historic destiny. In pre-Union times, the Scots had been divided against themselves between Royalist and Covenanter, Highlander and Lowlander, Jacobite and Whig. In an endeavour to display an even handed approach to the protagonists, Scott showed the good qualities in both sides of a divided Scotland. Scots were loyal, principled and heroic. Yet, such qualities went to waste in futile self-conflict. Pre-Union Scotland was very much a nation, a good nation, but one that was perpetually divided. The Union diverted Scotland away from internal division and those characteristic could now be put to good use in the service of the British state and Empire. In the eighteenth century Scottish history was depicted as a sordid tale of feudalism, backwardness and poverty.[29] By the early nineteenth century this history was given a new perspective to make it more positive. The backwardness and poverty of the past, it was argued, made the Scots more ambitious and thrusting in their desire to accumulate wealth and prosperity. The hardy climate of the Highlands and centuries of perpetual clan warfare had acted as an imperial kindergarten and produced the finest troops in the British Empire. Scotland's internal divisions and wars were evidence of the high principles that people believed in. Although the basic facts remained the same, the gloss that was put on them was altogether more favourable. In the 1850s, it was decided to erect a monument to Sir William Wallace to remind the Scots of their distinctive history. Sir Walter Scott put the regalia of Scotland on show in Edinburgh castle with the same objective in mind. In a changing world in which the distinctive national qualities of the nation were believed to be disappearing, many sought refuge in the past. Yet, it was a heavily romanticised and hazy past which bordered on the mythical. In the minds of the middle-class, the cosy view of Scotland located in a rural, pre-industrial setting was altogether more comforting than the reality of one of the fastest urbanising and industrialising societies in Europe.[30]

A second defining element in the reinvention of Scottish national identity in the early nineteenth century was the manufacture of an ideological canon of values which were presented as being intrinsically Scottish. Such values were centred upon laissez faire individualism and encompassed thrift, temperance, the work ethic, respectability and notions of meritocracy. In short, they were the ideals which found their best embodiment in the work of Haddington's Samuel Smiles, whose *Self-Help* acted as text book for Victorian middle-class aspirations.[31] Although laissez faire individualism was part and parcel of the forces of modernisation and industrialisation which were transforming Scottish society and in the minds of many, reducing Scotland to a mere province of England, its repackaging as traditional Scottish values added to its credibility. By arguing that such values had always been present in Scottish society, laissez faire individualism could be presented as traditional and as such, not a threat to Scottish national identity. Not surprisingly, such values were thrown back on the Scottish past. The cult of Sir William Wallace was based on notions that he was a man of the people who had come to the nation's rescue when the aristocracy had betrayed the national cause. Wallace owed his position not to birth, but to talent and ability. Although the middle class had attained the vote after 1832, much of Scottish society was still in the grip of aristocratic power, the conflict of patronage in the church being the most obvious example. Wallace was reinvented to give credibility to middle-class aspirations and their own struggles and ambitions were thrown back on the Scottish past. Similar cases and parallels were drawn with Robert Burns. Likewise a man of the people who owed his fame to his own talent and endeavours rather than noble birth.[32] The Covenanters and their fight for religious liberty and Presbyterian democracy acted as an example to those combating patronage in the Church.[33]

The notion of the 'lad o' pairts' was a major factor in the construction of an individualistic laissez fair cultural hegemony. The belief that Scottish society was inherently meritocratic and that social mobility was dependent on individual endeavour became one of the most pervasive of all Scottish myths.[34] Thomas Carlyle and David Livingstone were two shining examples that all Scots should seek to emulate. They vindicated the belief that hard effort would be rewarded and legitimised the validity of individualist values. The dominance of laissez faire ideology in Scotland was reflected in the political system by overwhelming support for the Liberal Party. With only a few exceptions, the party dominated Scottish politics from 1832 to 1914. Indeed, the notions of meritocracy was such that the Conservatives found it near impossible to shake off the stigma of landlordism, aristocratic privilege and reaction which for the most part confined them to the political backwaters in Scotland. Few issues commanded as much support in Scottish political circles as anti aristocratic sentiment and indeed, as late as the nineteen thirties, it formed an important part of the Labour Party's rhetoric.[35] Central government played little part in the day to day running of nineteenth century Scotland as power was devolved to local government boards which dealt with poor relief and education. The presence of British govenment rarely impinged on Scottish society. Nor, could not be said that the Scots felt remote from British government. Before the First World War, it was a source of pride that so many prime ministers had been Scottish. In 1879, Gladstone, who was of Scottish parentage, chose to restart his political career in the Mid-Lothian by election where his campaign of mid-Victorian morality chimed in harmony with the electorates expectations. The Grand Old Man seemed to encapsulate many of the values that the Scots believed to be intrinsic to their society.[36]

While much attention has focused on what divided Scotland in the nineteenth century, less attention has been paid to what united them. Although much ink has been spilled on the often obscurant debate which governed Scottish ecclesiastical and educational politics, it should not detract from the fact that there was an ideological hegemony of laissez faire values which permeated the whole of Scottish society. The very fact the Liberal Party had such overwhelming support makes the point and that concentration on the fractious nature of church factionalism in many ways could be described as fine tuning rather than outright division. Presbyterianism was central to this vision of Scottish identity. The proliferation of popular works commemorating the deeds of the Covenanters was supported by all the religious factions. Indeed, much of the debate was generated by competing claims to be the true heirs of the Covenanters. Presbyterianism was ideally suited to laissez fair nations of egalitarian meritocracy. The values of thrift, hard work, respectability and independence chimed in nicely with the perception of the covenanting tradition.[37]

By boalderising the essence of Scotland into symbolic representations which were located in a quasi mythical past and in a quasi mythical rural setting and by presenting the norms of Victorian values as essentially Scottish values, much was done to paper over the geographic, class and religious divisions in Scotland. Furthermore, by shifting the emphasis away from the traditional Scottish institutions and presenting the essence of Scottish nationality as identification with symbolic representations of the nation, much of the previously exclusive character of Scottish national identity was removed. By simply identifying with Highland scenery, the novels of Walter Scott, tartan, Robert Burns, the lad o' parts myth, hard work, Presbyterian democracy etc., one could become Scottish. This was, in a curious sense, more egalitarian and open to all who wanted it. The communications revolution considerably aided this process as the symbolic representations of Scottish nationhood were speedily transmitted throughout society.

Scotland and the Imperial Mission

Paradoxically, for most Scots the best place the display and demonstrate these characteristics which were thought to form the essence of Scottish national identity was outside Scotland. The British Empire was seen by most Scottish politicians and intellectuals as the logical culmination of the Union. It was argued time and time again that the *imperial partnership* was the result of the dynamic mix of the best qualities of the Scots and the English. As far as the Scots were concerned, the birth of the Empire dated from the Union and its creation was due as much to their own efforts as those of England. Indeed, some even attributed the loss of the American colonies in the eighteenth century to English neglect.[38] For many Scots, the imperial mission was Scotland's historic destiny.

As stated earlier, British imperialism was not monolithic and provided ample opportunity for the expression of the sub nationalisms of the British state. Imperial activity did much to reinforce and promote ideas of Scottish national identity and national characteristics. Indeed, the attributes commonly attributed to English imperialist sentiment have corresponding counterparts in nineteenth century Scotland. The essence of British imperial sentiment is to be found in a set of ideological clusters, such as militarism, monarchism, economic and religious expansionism and colonialism and for each of these, there was a distinctive Scottish contribution.

It was a matter of fundamental political faith in Scotland that the Scots enjoyed joint ownership of the Empire with England. Far from being peripheral to the development of British imperialism, Scottish politicians argued that their nation was essential to the process of British global expansion:

> Union has been mutually beneficial, a good thing for Scotland, but a better thing for England. Since the Union, our colonial Empire has been developed, and that Empire has been built up by Scottish blood and treasure, as by English.[39]

On the surface, there appeared to be no shortage of evidence to make good such claims. Glasgow was the 'Second city of the Empire' and Scottish businessmen were prominent in imperial economic activity. Scottish regiments played a major role in its conquest and defence. Scottish colonial governor generals administered large swathes of the Empire's territories, while the sons of the middle-class held important imperial civil service posts. Scots emigrants founded large parts of the Dominion colonies. The Scottish religious revolution was exported overseas as Presbyterianism was planted by Scots missionaries all over the globe. The Scottish public was told that since the mid eighteenth century:

> Scotsmen, whether as soldiers, statesmen, financiers, bankers, scientists, missionaries, physicians, preachers, journalists, educators, engineers, or merchants, have in all our Colonies fully held their own, nay, risen to positions of eminence.[40]

And although the Scots had no direct political control of their nation, this was of little consequence, as they took more interest in the fact that they were too busy ruling huge territories overseas. The Scots portrayed themselves as natural rulers and governers and this was used to explain why they had contributed so many Prime Ministers to the British nation. For example, some patriots complained bitterly at the tendency to describe Gladstone as English because both his parents had been Scots.[41] In such ways Scottish national self-esteem was raised to new heights and the popular perception of being a race of empire builders was born.

Undoubtedly, the military contribution of the Scottish regiments was the most important factor in the propagation of a distinctive Scottish input into British imperial activity. Scots soldiers served with distinction throughout the Empire and reinforced notions regarding the martial prowess of the Scottish race.[42] Scottish loyalty and tenacity were described as imbued racial characteristics which made the Scots natural soldiers. Heroic tales of regimental activities in the Napoleonic wars, Crimea, Afghanistan, Ashantee, Egypt and South Africa were recounted at home to show the special qualities of Scottish courage and loyalty.[43] The Scottish military input reinforced the belief that a distinct Scottish national dimension was at work in the creation of the Empire. 'Scotland for ever' was the battle cry of the illustrious Scots Greys who captured a French eagle at Waterloo and Cobbett's claim that the 42nd had not turned the tide against the French at the battle of Alexandria was met with a torrent of abuse, showing exactly how sensitive the Scots were when it came to matters concerning their military prowess.[44] Sir Colin Campbell illustrated this imperial Scottish nationalism when addressing veterans of the Alma in 1855:

> Remember to never lose sight of the circumstance that you are natives of Scotland; that your country admires you for your bravery; that it still expects much from you; in short let every one consider himself a hero of Scotland.... For your deeds on that day you have received the marked encomiums of Lord Raglan, the thanks of the Queen, and the admiration of all. Scotchmen are proud of you.[45]

A host of Scottish generals were praised for their leadership qualities and the fact that most Scottish regiments were commanded by Scottish officers reinforced the national dimension. General Gordon's martyrdom at Khartoum in 1886 raised his stature to almost mythical heights: 'General Gordon was one who even by then had saved an Empire, and had rescued, by his own individual example and force of character, a whole population from massacre and devastation'.[46] In the Nile Campaign of 1898, the Queen's Own Camerionian Highlanders were congratulated by Victoria on their gallantry, suffering half of the total British casualties and her journals reveal, as well as a great fondness, an appreciation of the distinctive qualities of the Scottish militia.[47] Regular reports in the Scottish press kept the public informed of their soldiers' campaigns, reinforcing the notion that the Empire was as much theirs as it was England's. By allowing the Scots such a high profile military input, the British Empire encouraged and promoted Scottish militarism; a vital component of any expansionist nationalism.

The role of Scottish settlers and administrators in the Empire was another source of Scottish self-congratulation. The fact that the Scots emigrated to Canada, New Zealand, Australia and South Africa was interpreted as a sign of national virility and prowess, rather than the result of grim social and economic opportunities at home.[48] Furthermore, because so many of the émigré Scots communities kept in touch with the mother country and, more often than not, reinforced their identification with the symbols of Scottish nationality, this popular image of the Scottish Diaspora was enhanced. As Lord Strathcona, the High Commissioner for Canada put it:

> Scotsmen in the Colonies retain that pride of country which is innate in the race. Scottish literature, Scottish poetry, and Scottish song retain their hold upon the people as much as, perhaps more than, they do at home. All these mean much to the Scotsman away from his native land. [49]

Not only were the Scots distinctive in their nationality, they were also noted for their success. As Sir Charles Dilke put it: 'In British settlements ...for every Englishman you meet who has worked himself up to wealth from small beginnings without external aid, you find ten Scotchmen'.[50] The jubilation which greeted the appointment of a Scottish aristocrat to the post of a colonial governor was another

indication of the popular esteem with which the Scottish contribution
to the Empire was held. The activities of lords Elgin, Dalhousie,
Argyll and Minto were regularly reported in the Scottish press.[51] As
John MacKenzie has pointed out, almost a third of the colonial
governor generals in the period from 1850 to 1939 were Scots, which
by any reckoning, is a disproporionate influence.[52] The Empire was
likewise of critical importance as an outlet for the talents of the
Scottish professional classes. Lawyers, engineers, academics, teachers,
doctors and ministers all found their calling in imperial service. As the
New Zealand prime minister, Joseph Ward, put it: 'their friends from
the old land had carried into the new one of New Zealand the arts,
sciences and commerce that they were taught before they went from
Scotland'. [53]

Scottish missionaries, likewise played an important role in projecting
Scottish national identity out onto the world stage. David Livingstone
became an object of hero worship in the Victorian period because he
seemed to be the embodiment of Scottish virtue.[54] His lowly origins
were cited as evidence of the meritocratic nature of Scottish society
and the superiority of Scottish education. His zeal and determination
were cited in numerous popular publications as quintessential Scottish
characteristics which youngsters should seek to emulate. For many, he
was the most striking example of the fact that 'Scotland did certainly
produce wonderful men.'[55] Livingstone was the inspiration behind
numerous overseas missions and much of the Free Church and
established Church's efforts were directed towards this area. In 1875
the Free Church established its Livingstonia Mission, while the
established church founded its Blantyre Mission the following year,
both evidently in pursuit of the claim to be Livingstone's spiritual heir.[56]
Overseas work was important because it drew attention away from the
problems of division at home. Also, it helped to inject new vigour and
glamour into the Presbyterian mission which was seen to be faltering
due to the problems of urbanisation.[57]

Scotland's economic position within the Empire was of critical
importance in contributing to the Scottish imperial identity. The
Empire was clearly recognised as the source of Scottish wealth,
although the critical factor was the Scots ability to exploit these
opportunities:

what was the secret of the marvellous success of the Scottish
people during the last century in Scotland itself, in England and
in the outer Britains? ... their poverty was equal to their
patriotism: their energy to both. How did they succeed? By
intense industry, by severe frugality, by constant adaptability to
all circumstances and all conditions, however rigorous and novel
they might be. And so it was that they raised Scotland to wealth
and Scotsmen to power. [58]

Tea and plantation merchants, shipping orders to the Empire and Royal
Navy, locomotives for imperial service, oil and rubber merchants,
financial investment and textile products all located the Scottish
economy firmly within the imperial nexus.[59] Sir William Mackinnon
founded the Imperial British East Africa Company which was
instrumental in expanding the Empire into East Africa. The
proliferation of rotary societies in the guise of the British Empire Club
clearly revealed the economic priority of the Scottish middle-class.[60]

The notion that the Scots were a race of empire builders and had
an imperial destiny to fulfil was common currency in Scottish domestic
political circles. Indeed, much effort was made in cultivating and
promoting the idea of a Scottish imperial mission:

It is not because Scotland is united with England that the
Scotchman should forget the glories of his annals, or relax one
jot in his love for his native soil. I say this not to flatter you- I say
it for Scotland alone. I say it for the sake of the Empire.[61]

The sanctity of the imperial ethos crossed political divides and was
universally accepted. Radical Liberals extolled the virtues of sane
imperialism and pointed to the superiority of the British Empire in
comparison to other colonial powers.[62] British overseas government
was enlightened and principled and brought the benefits of an advanced
civilisation. For the Scots, they played an important role in this
development by bringing to the Empire their 'rich contribution of
culture and heritage' and it was often claimed that the Scots had a
special talent when it came to communicating with the native peoples.[63]

Indeed, the Scots had a propensity to take the moral high ground on imperial affairs with major petitions launched against the Jamaican outrages and support for Gladstone against the evils of Beaconsfieldism, in which the Conservative prime minister, Disraeli, was accused of whipping up jingoistic sentiment for his own political purposes.[64] Lord Rosebery frequently extolled the Scottish characteristics of trust, loyalty and hard work which had made the Scottish contribution to the creation of the Empire so noticeable and so natural. For many Scots, imperial service was a Scottish national duty, as Rosebery put it to the student body of Edinburgh University:

> If the students could remain in Edinburgh and concentrate themselves here, it would be bad for Edinburgh and bad for Scotland, but bad also for Empire. We in Scotland wish to continue to mould the Empire as we have in the past - and we have not moulded it by stopping at home....You will, when you go forth from these learned precincts and enter the actual business of life- you will in the course of your lives help maintain and build the Empire ... this Edinburgh ... though it may not be the capital of the Empire, is yet, in the sense of the sacrifices that it has made and in the generations of men that it has given to the Empire, in the truest, and highest and largest sense an Imperial City.[65]

Scottish racial characteristics were frequently cited as being instrumental in their predisposition towards empire building. Lamarkian and social Darwinian notions of evolution in a harsh climate and environment were often cited as being responsible for shaping the hardy, determined and adaptable Scottish character.[66] According to Rosebery in one of his most quoted phrases: 'An Empire such as ours requires as its first condition an imperial race -a race vigorous and industrious and intrepid' and the Scots seemed to fit the bill, after all, it was an address to a Scottish audience.[67] Conservatives were likewise equally trenchant in their support of the empire, with Sir Henry Craik and Lord Balfour of Burleigh stating that imperial service was the highest principle that any Scot could hope to attain.[68] The Jacobite martial qualities and loyalty to the bitter end were represented as quintessential Scottish characteristics which were now effectively harnessed for service in the empire.[69] Even the Scottish Labour leader, Keir Hardie, supported the imperial mission:

> The indomitable pluck and energy of the British people had carried the British flag all over the world and promised to make the British Empire the one great power that would mould the affairs of the world. He thought that this was right that this should be so.[70]

The Boys Brigade was formed in Glasgow in 1883 to promote Christianity and was heavily laden with imperial ideals.[71] The Volunteers were prominent in promoting militarism. They replicated the uniforms of the regular army and were frequently engaged in pageants, parades and exercises in the full glare of the public. The volunteers gave many Scots the opportunity to fulfil the fantasies of frustrated empire builders stuck at home. [72] The growth of popular literature which focused on imperial activities and heroes transmitted imperial values throughout society.[73] Queen Victoria's affair with her northern Kingdom contributed to her popularity in Scotland. Indeed, with her frequent and long visits, her fascination with all that was Highland and her fanciful statement that she was really a Jacobite at heart, all contributed to the notion that the Scots occupied a unique and special role within the British nations.[74] By decorating Scottish soldiers at Balmoral, attending the Scottish Church and patronising the Highland Games, it seemed for many Scots as though they had captured and reclaimed the monarchy for their own.

When Anglo Scottish tensions rose to the surface it was usually the result of English indifference to the Scottish contribution to the Empire. In many ways, the reaction to perceived English slights against the Scottish imperial contribution or Scotland's historic nationhood were the best illustrations of how deeply ingrained the notion of the imperial partneship was in Scottish society. The use of 'England' and 'English' instead of 'British' and 'Britain' brought forth numerous complaints from the Scots:

Scotland's claim to honourable fulfilment of these Treaty obligations (The Treaty of Union which stipulated the use of Britain and British) becomes the stronger when Scotland's share in the work of the United kingdom is considered ... Our Highland Regiments which have fought so valiantly in every part of the world, did so to maintain the honour, not of England, but the United kingdom. Go where you may, and you will find Scotsmen occupying foremost places, and doing more than their proportionate share in adding to the lustre and dignity of the British name ... in regard to loyalty, we owe none to England, and never did. Our loyalty is due to the British Crown and British Government.[75]

Even the Eton and Oxford educated Scottish Secretary, Balfour of Burleigh, was forced to intervene from time to time in order to insist that 'Scotland might be mentioned as an integral portion of the Empire'.[76] Indeed, he had to prevent the removal of the Scottish Crown to London for an exhibition as this offended Scottish sensibilities and was tireless in his efforts to persuade the prime minister, Salisbury, to use 'British' rather than 'English'.[77] His exasperation with English insensitivity to Scottish national sentiment clearly showed over the refusal of Anglican Churches in India to allow Presbyterian services:

it took something more than a surgical operation to get it into the head of the average Englishman that Scotland was a nation with national feelings, national pride and national rights... If the English mind in India would insist on regarding Scotland as a foreign country, they must have an ambassador properly accredited, so that they might have their view put forward by the spoken word. [78]

The decision of the new monarch to style himself Edward VII in 1903 was believed to be an insult to Scotland because it ignored the Scottish royal line and the fact that there had never been a king Edward of Scotland. Not only was it insensitive, it undermined the notion of the imperial partnership. The Scots were nonplussed and made their feelings known, as the *Times* sardonically noted:

the snub administered to them (the King and Queen) by the Convention of Burghs, which is nothing if it is not truly and characteristically Scottish: their influence is no less unmistakable in the resolution of several public bodies to omit the 'numeral' from the inscription on their coronation medals, and in the untimely fits of economy that have overcome some authorities not as a rule averse to feasting. [79]

The Loyal address by the Church of Scotland contained no reference to the numeral and none were to be found when the King visited Glasgow in May 1903. Further outrage towards English insensitivity to Scotland's imperial role occurred in 1906 when it was decided to move the headquarters of the Scots Greys to England. A protest meeting was addressed by Rosebery, who did not mince his words:

We in Scotland are treated as if we were of no account at all. Is our nationality of no importance to the army? I hold that if you take Scotland out of your military history you will have to cut out some of the most precious pages in the volume ... Are we always to be treated as the Milk Cow of the Empire? Are we simply to be milked and receive nothing in return? [80]

Hostility did arise from time to time, but usually occurred as a result of injured pride and had little to do with animosity to the British imperial ideal. Indeed, it hurt all the more for being such blatant reminders that the Scots were the junior partners in the imperial mission.

When discussing the Union and Scottish politics in the latter part of the nineteenth century and well into the twentieth century, it has to be borne in mind that many in Scottish society had come to see the Empire and their role in it as the natural outgrowth of the treaty which was signed in 1707. In essence, the Union and the Empire were part and parcel of the grand British design. When politicians talked about reform and development of government in Scotland it was usually linked to ideas concerning the imperial structure. After all, the Empire played such an important part in defining Scottish self-perception. Yet, this identity and the political system within which it operated were

largely middle-class constructs. Imperial sentiment, laissez faire
ideology and a rosy, sentimental view of Scotland and the Scottish
past, however, had little to do with the daily experience of most Scots.
Indeed, as will be seen in the next chapter, political discourse on the
government of Scotland and the Union after 1880 was largely
influenced by changes within Scottish society. The romantic, imperial
and backward looking vision of Scottish identity was losing its
relevance in a society which was becoming more and more
preoccupied with the inward realities of an urban and industrial society.

NOTES

[1] See E.H.H. Green, *The Crisis of Conservatism: the politics, economics and
ideology of the British Conservative Party, 1880-1914*, (London, 1995), pp.
27-59.

[2] There is an extensive literature covering these themes. See Green, *Crisis of
Conservatism;* G.R. Searle, *The Quest for National Efficiency, 1899-1914*,
(London, 1990); A. Sykes, *Tariff Reform in British Politics*, (Oxford, 1979);
M. Bentley, *The Climax of Liberal Politics: British Liberalism in Theory
and Practice 1868-1918* and R. Jay, *Joseph Chamberlain: A Political Study*
(Oxford, 1981).

[3] H.V. Emy, *Liberals, Radicals and Social Politics, 1892-1914*, (Cambridge,
1973) and M. Freeden, *The New Liberalism: An Ideology of Social Reform*,
(Oxford, 1978).

[4] See W.H. Greenleaf, *The British Political Tradition, vol. I The Rise of
Collectivism*, (London, 1983) and M. Fforde, *Conservatism and
Collectivism, 1886-1914*, (Edinburgh, 1990).

[5] For the Liberal Party on this issue see H.C.G. Matthew, *The Liberal
Imperialists*, (London, 1973).

[6] Green, *The Crisis of Conservatism.*

[7] Sykes, *Tariff Reform.*

[8] See J.M. MacKenzie, 'Essay and Reflection: Scotland and the British
Empire', *International History Review*, 4 (1993), pp. 714-39; R.J. Finlay,
'The Rise and Fall of Popular Imperialism in Scotland 1850-1950', *Scottish
Geographical Magazine*, 113 (1997), pp. 13-21 and R.J. Finlay, 'Imperial

Scotland: The British Empire and Scottish National Identity, c. 1850-1914', in J.M. MacKenzie (ed), *Studies in Imperialism: Scotland and the British Empire*, (Manchester, forthcoming)..

[9] In particular J.M. MacKenzie, *Propaganda and Empire: the Manipulation of British Public Opinion, 1880-1960*, (Manchester, 1984) and P. J. Cains & A.G. Hopkins, *British Imperialism, vol. I Innovation and Expansion, 1688-1914, vol. II Crisis and Deconstruction, 1914-1990*, (London, 1993).

[10] R. Hyam, *Britain's Imperial Century, 1815-1914*, (London, 1993 edition), pp. 1-8.

[11] Finlay, 'Popular Imperialism; MacKenzie, 'Scotland and the British Empire' and Keith Jeffery (ed), *An Irish Empire? Aspects of Ireland and the British Empire*, (Manchester, 1996).

[12] T.M. Devine, 'Introduction' in T.M. Devine & R. Mitchison (eds), *People and Society in Scotland, 1760-1830*, (Edinburgh, 1988), pp. 1-9.

[13] I.G.C. Hutchison, *A Political History of Scotland, 1832-1924: Parties, Elections and Issues*, (Edinburgh, 1986), p. 1.

[14] See S.J. Brown, *Thomas Chalmers and the Godly Commonwealth*, (Oxford, 1982); C. Brown, *The Social History of Religion in Scotland Since 1730*, (London, 1987) and S.J. Brown & M.Fry (eds), *Scotland in the Age of Disruption*, (Edinburgh, 1993).

[15] Brown, *Thomas Chalmers*, pp. 278-9.

[16] See D.J. Withrington, 'Scotland a Half Educated Nation in 1843? Reliable Critique or Persuasive polemic' in W.Humes and H.M. Patterson (eds), *Scottish Culture and Scottish Education*, (Edinburgh, 1983), pp. 57-75.

[17] R.D. Anderson, *Education and Opportunity in Victorian Scotland*, (Edinburgh, 1989), pp. 27-70.

[18] N. Phillipson, *The Scottish Whigs and the Reform of the Court of Session, 1785-1830*, (Edinburgh, 1990).

[19] W. Ferguson, 'The Reform Act (Scotland): Intention and Effect', *Scottish Historical Review*, 45 (1965), pp. 105-16.

[20] Finlay, 'Popular Imperialism', pp. 14-15.

[21] NLS, The Scottish rights association, NE 20, 13-14, book 1, p.3.

[22] *Times*, 4 Dec. 1856.

[23] NLS, The Scottish rights association, book 1, p.78.

[24] *Glasgow Sentinel*, 19 Nov. 1853.

[25] *ibid.*

[26] T.Nairn, *The Break-Up of Britain*, (London, 1981), p. 162.

[27] R.J. Finlay, 'Myths, Heroes and Anniversaries in Modern Scotland', *Scottish Affairs*, 18 (1997), pp. 108-126 and R.J. Finlay, 'The Burns Cult and

Scottish Identity in the Nineteenth and Twentieth Centuries' in K. Simpson (ed), *Love and Liberty: Robert Burns, a bicentenary celebration*, (Edinburgh, 1997).

[28] See T.M. Devine, *Clanship to Crofters' War*, (Manchester, 1994), pp. 84-100 and R. Clyde, *From Rebel to Hero: The Image of the Highlander, 1745-1830*, (Edinburgh, 1995).

[29] Colin Kidd, *Subverting Scotland's Past: Scottish Whig Historians and the Creation of an Anglo British Identity, 1689- c.!830*, (Cambridge, 1993).

[30] R.J. Finlay, 'Controlling the Past: Scottish Historiography and Scottish Identity in the 19th and 20th Centuries', *Scottish Affairs*, 9 (1994), pp. 127-43.

[31] A.Calder, 'Livingstone, Self-Help and Scotland', in J.M. MacKenzie (ed), *David Livingstone and the Victorian Encounter with Africa*, (London, 1996), pp. 79-108.

[32] See Finlay, 'Myths, Heroes and Anniversaries' and R.J. Finlay, 'The Burns Cults'.

[33] James Begg, *A Violation of the Treaty of Union: The Main Origin of our Ecclesiastical Divisions and other Evils*, (Edinburgh, 1871).

[34] D. McCrone, *Understanding Scotland: the Sociology of a Stateless Nation*, (London, 1992).

[35] M. Fry, *Patronage and Principle: A Political History of Modern Scotland*, (Aberdeen, 1987), pp. 88-119.

[36] J.G. Kellas, 'The Liberal Party in Scotland, 1876-95', *Scottish Historical Review*, 44 (1965), pp. 1-16.

[37] The following are just some of the titles to be found in the catalogue of John Ritchie, publisher of Christian literature; *Heroes and Heroines of the Covenanters, Martyrs of the Moors, Tales and Sketches of the Scottish Covenanters, Helen of the Glen* and *Men of the Covenant*.

[38] NLS, Scottish Home Rule Association Pamphlets, c.1890, *A protest against the mis-use of the terms 'England' and 'English' for 'Britain'*, *its empire, its people and institutions*, p. 2.

[39] *H.C. Debs.*, vol. 335, col. 114, 9 April 1889.

[40] C.W. Thomson, *Scotland's Work and Worth*, (Edinburgh, no date, c. 1908), p.733.

[41] David Forsyth, "Empire and Union: Imperialism and National Identity in Nineteenth Century Scotland', *Scottish Geographical Magazine*, 113 (1997), pp. 6-13.

[42] There is a huge literature on this and some examples are; James Logan, *The Scottish Gael*, (Inverness, 1876); General Sir Bruce Tulloch,

Recollections of Forty Years Service, (Edinburgh, 1904); John Scott Keltie, *A history of the Scottish Highlands' Clans and Highland Regiments*, (Edinburgh, 1877).

[43] *ibid.;* Thomson, *Work and Worth*, pp. 598-621; J. Stirling, *Our Regiments in South Africa, 1899-1902*, (London, 1904); H. Davidson, *History and Service of the 78th Highlanders*, (Edinburgh, 1901); S. Howie, *A History of the 1st Lanarkshire Volunteers*, (Glasgow, 1887) and J. Ritchie, *Brave Deeds of British Boys*, (Kilmarnock, 1890).

[44] D. Green (ed), *Cobbett's Tour in Scotland*, (Aberdeen, 1984), pp. 141-42. See also the *Scotsman*, 17 Nov. 1906 for an account of the unveiling of the memorial to the Scots Greys.

[45] *Scotsman*, 21 Sep. 1855.

[46] The Duke of Argyll, *Scotland as it was and as it is*, (Edinburgh, 1887), p. 465.

[47] *Scotsman*, 14 Nov. 1898 and D. Duff (ed), *Queen Victoria's Highland Journals*, (Exeter, 1980), pp. 24-5; 220-25.

[48] J.H. Burton, *The Scot Abroad*, (Edinburgh, 1881), pp. 1-22 and J.Ker, *Scottish nationality and other papers*, (Edinburgh, 1887), p. 213.

[49] Quoted in Thomson, *Work and Worth*, p. 755. Further examples can be found in G. Donaldson, *The Scots Overseas*, (London 1966), pp. 103-94 and C. Cumming, 'Scottish National Identity in an Australian Colony', *Scottish Historical Review*, 72 (1993), pp. 22-38.

[50] Sir Charles Dilke, *Greater Britain*, (London, 1888), p. 525.

[51] For example see the *Scotsman*, Feb. 1894 on the appointment of Lord Elgin as Governor General of India.

[52] MacKenzie, 'Scotland and the British Empire'.

[53] Quoted Thomson, *Work and Worth*, p. 792.

[54] J.M. MacKenzie, 'David Livingstone: The Construction of the Myth', in G.Walker & T. Gallagher (eds), *Sermons and Battle Hymns: Protestant Popular Culture in Modern Scotland*, (Edinburgh, 1990), pp. 24-33.

[55] J.B. Mackie, *The Life and Work of Duncan McLaren*, (Edinburgh, 1888), vol. II, p. 78, which has details of the unveiling of Livingstone's memorial in Edinburgh.

[56] R. Hunter, *History of the Foreign Missions of the Free Church of Scotland in India and Africa*, (London, 1873).

[57] Hugh Miller, 'The Effects of Religious Disunion on Colonisation', in John Davidson (ed), *Hugh Miller: Notes and Essays*, (Edinburgh, 1870), pp. 221-131. Also, Brown and Fry (eds), *Scotland in the Age of Disruption*.

[58] Lord Rosebery, 'Questions of Empire: An Address Delivered as Lord Rector to the Students of Glasgow University, November 16, 1900', in John Buchan (ed), *Lord Rosebery: Miscellanies, Literary and Historical*, (London, 1921), vol. II, 252.

[59] See B.P. Lenman, *An Economic History of Modern Scotland*, (London, 1977), pp. 167-193.

[60] C.C. Lee, 'The Victorian Business Community in Glasgow, c. 1840-1870', University of Strathclyde Ph.D. (1985), pp. 378-400.

[61] Sir E. Bulwer Lytton, *Edinburgh News*, Jan. 1854.

[62] See Matthews, *The Liberal Imperialist*, for the influence of Scotland on the development of Liberal Imperialism. Also, T. Shaw, *Patriotism and the Empire*, (Edinburgh, 1903).

[63] For some examples of see A.D. Gibb, *Scottish Empire*, (1937), pp. 113, 241, 248.

[64] Mackie, *Life of McLaren*, p. 75 for the petition against the Jamaican massacres. D. Brookes, 'Gladstone and Midlothian', *Scottish Historical Review*, 64 (1985), pp. 42-67.

[65] Rosebery, 'The Service of the State: Presidential Address to the Associated Societies of the University of Edinburgh, 25 Oct. 1898', in Buchan (ed), *Rosebery: Miscellanies*, vol. II, p. 195.

[66] For example, see Argyll, *Scotland as it was and as it is*, pp. 475-483 and Ker, *Scottish Nationality*, pp. 1-7.

[67] Rosebery, 'Questions of Empire', p. 250..

[68] Sir Henry Craik, *A Century of Scottish History: From the Days Before the 45 to those within Living Memory*, (Edinburgh, 1901), vol. I, p.18 and Lady Frances Balfour, *Lord Balfour of Burleigh*, (London, 1924), p. 83.

[69] See Finlay, 'Myths, Heroes and Anniversaries'.

[70] Quotes in F. Reid, *Keir Hardie: The Making of a Socialist*, (London, 1978), p. 124.

[71] See John Springhall, Brian Fraser & Michael Hoare, *Sure and Steadfast: A History of the Boys Brigade, 1883 to 1983*, (London, 1983).

[72] Hugh Cunningham, *The Volunteer Force*, (London, 1978); G.H. Smith, *With the Scottish Rifle Volunteers to the Front*, (Glasgow, 1901) and J.H. Watson, *Military Glasgow*, (Glasgow, 1895).

[73] See Finlay 'Popular Imperialism'. Some examples of popular literature which had a heavy imperial content were; *Volunteer Gazette; North British Daily Mail; B.B. Gazettte* and *Deeds That Won an Empire*.

[74] Duff, *Queen Victoria's Highland Journals*, p. 25.

[75] Scottish Home Rule Association, *A protest against the misuse of the terms*, p. 3.
[76] Lady Balfour, *Balfour*, pp. 89-95.
[77] *ibid.* p. 93.
[78] Quoted in Thomson, *Scotland's Worth and Work*, p. 573.
[79] *Times*, 21 May 1903.
[80] *Scotsman*, 4 Dec. 1906.

CHAPTER TWO

Scottish Home Rule and the Rise of Progressivism, 1880-1914

Scottish home rule emerged as an issue in Scottish politics in the 1880s as a result of three factors. Firstly, it was part and parcel of a wider debate generated by increasing demands that government ought to play a greater role in Scottish society and devote more time and attention to its problems. The Scots felt short-changed when they compared the limited amount of attention they received when contrasted with the problem child of the Empire, Ireland. Truculent Irish MPs disrupted parliamentary business and a seemingly inordinate amount of parliamentary time was spent trying to resolve that nation's grievances.[1] There grew a widespread feeling that Scotland was being usurped from the special niche that it had carved out in British politics because of the antics of Irish home rulers. After all, the Scots acted as model citizens of the Empire, whereas the Irish were perceived as being rewarded by a welter of special legislation on account of their obstinate and, at times, terrorist, behaviour. As Lord Rosebery put it: 'Justice for Ireland means everything is done for her even to the payment of her native's debts. Justice to Scotland means insulting neglect. I leave for Scotland next week with the view of blowing up a prison or shooting a policeman.'[2] While Ireland basked in the limelight of British political attention, the Scots had to make do with a mere six hours of parliamentary time a year. A second, and closely related factor, in the emergence of Scottish home rule demand was the situation in Ireland. Gladstone's conversion to Irish home rule in 1886 raised important issues as to the future government of the British state and Empire and how Scotland would fit into the new scheme of things. For many Scots, it seemed unthinkable that Ireland should receive special treatment ahead of Scotland and if anything, it was Scotland which was best placed to exercise responsible home rule. Indeed, many harked back to Gladstone's pronouncement made in Aberdeen in 1871 that: 'If the doctrine of home rule is to be established in Ireland, I protest, on your behalf, that you will be just as well entitled to it in Scotland, and moreover, I protest on behalf of Wales, that it will be entitled to home rule also.'[3] If Ireland was good enough for home rule, then so was Scotland. A third factor in stirring up demand for Scottish home rule was undoubtedly increasing nationalist sentiment. The 1880s have been identified as a time when English national identity was becoming more populist and in this process, Scotland was excluded.[4] Popular English nationalism irritated many Scots, especially when 'England' and 'Britain' were used as undifferentiated terms.   The London-centric view of Empire was another source of grievance and the period witnessed the setting up of a plethora of organisations which would reinforce the notion of Scotland as a separate and distinctive contributor to the British imperial mission. London's lion's share of imperial expenditure led many to complain that Scotland was being mistreated.[5]

Home rule seemed an ideal panacea for these problems. It would halt the legislative neglect of Scotland. It could provide the Empire with a new and vibrant form of government which would allow the imperial parliament in London to concentrate on the important matters of state while leaving domestic legislatures to deal with their own concerns. Home rule held the promise of satisfying Ireland's sense of national grievance. Also, it could provide an outlet for the expression of Scottish national sentiment. While it is possible to identify these distinct strands in the progress of Scottish home rule sentiment, the problem facing the historian is that these issues formed a complex web in which different people with different interests put different emphasis on different aspects of the policy at different times.

The First Scottish Home Rule Movement

The issue of home rule emerged at a time of cultural regeneration in England. This vibrant and at times chauvinistic, English national identity brought forth complaints from many Scots who were appalled at English insensitivity to Scottish nationality. This was not a new phenomenon, but by the 1880s many Scots were speaking out against this. In the field of culture, many were incensed by the fact that England was hoarding the lion's share of government expenditure on galleries and museums.[6] This was all the more irritating when it was known that Scotland contributed by far and away a greater proportional sum to the Exchequer. Scotland, according to Rosebery, was the 'milch cow' of the Empire and was not getting her just deserts. In the 1890s formal complaints were issued against the Prime Minister,

Lord Salisbury, for his persistent use of England instead of Britain. The furore was such that the Scottish Secretary, Balfour of Burleight, wrote to him pleading to take account of the sensitivity of the Scots. Yet, it was all in vain as Salisbury could not see what the fuss was about.[7] Indeed, one of the first actions of the Scottish Home Rule Association, which was formed in 1886, was to issue a pamphlet entitled *A Protest against the mis-use of the terms 'England' and 'English' for 'Britain', its Empire, its people and its institutions.*

The Scots responded to this English insensitivity by demanding and giving greater prominence to Scottish national institutions. Interest in Scottish culture was given a boost and demands were made for chairs of Celtic and Scottish History in the universities. The foundation of the Scottish History Society in 1886 and the Scottish Geographical Society in 1884 were examples of the cultural defensiveness of the Scots. The endeavour to compete against British societies invariably ran into financial pressures. Funds for the Chairs in Scottish history and Celtic had to be raised at home and the persistent complaint was that English culture was subsidised by the exchequer to which the Scots paid a disproportionate share. National collections of scientific interest in Scotland were perennially under funded. The Scottish expedition to Antarctica by Dr Bruce in 1902 was paid largely by money raised at home. In 1914 the government refused to pay £3, 800 to complete publication of the scientific results which was contrasted with the funding of Scott and Shackleton's expeditions which together received more than £100,000. As was noted in chapter one, Anglo Scottish grievances were at their worse when English insensitivity failed to realise the notion of the imperial partnership and instead treated the Scots as a minor appendage. Yet, for all this, it did little to diminish the Scottish enthusiasm for promoting Scottish national institutions. The Glasgow Empire Exhibition of 1911 was an example of the belief that the Scots were a vibrant and distinctive national component of the Empire. The great work that went into institutions such as the Royal Society of Edinburgh, the National Library of Scotland, the National Museum of Scotland and others was testament of the desire by many Scots to create a cultural apparatus which would reinforce notions about Scotland's distinctive national identity. And, it has to be remembered, it was in this cultural climate that the issue of Scottish home rule was debated.

Irish home rule was the trigger which most historians have identified as being the catalyst which brought the debate on Scottish home rule in the 1880s to life.[8] Irish home rule instigated a fundamental re-assessment of the imperial ethos as contemporaries debated the future political structure of the Empire. At first the Scots were suspicious that the Irish would receive preferential treatment.[9] Also, Gladstone's endorsement of Irish home rule put the establishment of the Scottish Secretary in 1885 into the shade. The reinstatement of the office was designed to give greater prominence to Scottish affairs in the government and act as a symbol of Scottish nationhood. The demands for the post had been fuelled by a considerable amount of Scottish national sentiment and the campaign, orchestrated by Rosebery, had attracted a significant amount of cross party support.[10] Compared to home rule, the creation of a junior cabinet post was small beer indeed. At a stroke, the concessions given to Scotland were seen to be of little consequence.

The issue was compounded by the fact that the Irish were seen to be rewarded for engaging in terrorist activities, whereas the Scots, on account of their good behaviour, were delegated to second place. This caused considerable resentment. The issue split the Liberal Party in Scotland and even among some of the Liberal Unionists, who had seceded from the party in protest, there was a belief that home rule was more appropriate to Scotland. Irish home rule had brought nothing but acrimony in its wake. It had divided Scottish politics and even among those who were sympathetic to Ireland's cause, there was a sense that the issue was not worth the candle. The financial disparity of Scotland and Ireland with regard to payment to the Exchequer also hurt. The Scots paid in more than they got out, while the Irish paid in hardly anything but were treated as a special case. William Hunter MP claimed that the Scots were over taxed to the extent of £1, 100, 000 per year.[11] Whether this figure is accurate or not, it does reveal that many Scots felt that they were carrying a disproportionate share of the imperial burden. The assumption made by many historians that Irish and Scottish home rule were natural bedfellows is not borne out by the facts. Many Scottish home rulers resented the fact that Ireland was given priority and their literature often reflected this: 'The proposal to grant a Legislature and Executive government to Ireland, and withhold them from Scotland, is *unjust to a loyal, industrious and intelligent people, and appears to set a premium upon disorder'.*[12] If anybody deserved home rule it was the Scots and not the Irish.

It was in response to Gladstone's conversion to Irish home rule that the Scottish Home Rule Association was formed by Charles Waddie, John Romans, G.B. Clark, William Mitchell and others to campaign for the setting up of a Scottish parliament in Edinburgh.[13] The objectives of the Association were straight forward:

1. To promote the establishment of a legislature sitting in Scotland, with full control over all purely Scottish questions, and with an Executive government responsible to it and the crown.
2. To secure the government of Scotland, in the same degree as it is at present possessed by the Imperial government, the control of her Civil Servants, Judges, and other Officials, with the exception of those engaged in the military, naval and diplomatic services and collecting the Imperial revenue.
3. To maintain the integrity of the Empire, and secure that the voice of Scotland shall be heard in the Imperial Parliament as fully as at present when discussing Imperial Affairs.[14]

The Association was to attract a cross section of society; old radical Liberals who had been involved with the Association for the Vindication of Scottish Rights, the catholic aristocrat, the Marquis of Bute, pragmatists who were interested in home rule as a means to reform imperial government and a younger generation of Liberal MPs and Labour Party activists who believed some form of self-government would enable the more speedy creation of positive legislation for Scotland. The impetus for the movement had came from the older radical wing of the mid-nineteenth century Liberal Party. They dominated the Association's publications and held most of the official positions. Their views were often at conflict with more progressive elements in the Liberal Party. Temperance did not find any favour as some of the older members thought that it was their patriotic duty to drink whisky. Modern forms of popular culture such as the music hall and football, were denounced as the entertainment of the 'lower Saxon'.[15] Traditional Gladstonian attitudes to social policy permeated much of their thinking and there was a reluctance to abandon laissez faire in social policy. Landowners and the aristocracy received considerable flack and attention focused on the slights to Scottish nationhood, such as the flying of the Red Ensign by the Royal Navy. Such old fashioned, Mid-Victorian radicalism had little electoral appeal and tinted the Association with a somewhat cranky image which it would find hard to shake off. Indeed, by the Edwardian period, the Association was a spent force and progressive Liberals had turned to the Young Scots Society as the principal home rule organisation. In 1908, Waddie claimed that both main parties had betrayed Scotland and nothing seemed capable of shaking the Scots out of apathy.[16] Although some mainstream Liberal MPs were attracted to the notion of Scottish home rule, the idea remained somewhat ill-defined and it was difficult to package their ideas into a coherent form. This point was not lost by critics who repeatedly stressed, in contrast to claims to the contrary, that there was no popular support for Scottish home rule.[17] Although numerous Scottish home rule bills were introduced in the late Victorian period, the vagueness of the movement makes it difficult to distinguish how much of this was a genuine demand for home rule and how much of it was part and parcel of the campaign to improve the existing mechanisms of government in Scotland which had been started with the campaign for the reinstatement of a Scottish secretary. This question will be dealt with later.

Among many Scots who supported the principle of Irish home rule, it was recognised that a similar measure would be necessary for Scotland to keep things equal and maintain a unified structure for the Empire. Imperial Federation was the idea most widely endorsed because it seemed to offer a solution to the problems of parliamentary over-work by allowing national and dominion assemblies to deal with domestic legislation, which would leave Westminster free to concentrate on the more important issues of foreign and imperial policy.[18] It was pointed out that in the period 1900-1909 only about half of the bills mentioned in the King's speech were enacted into law. Numerous Scottish MPs claimed that the quality of Scottish legislation was poor simply because it received insufficient parliamentary time.

The 1890 Housing Act was found to be difficult to apply to Scotland. In 1898 a committee was appointed to inquire into procedure in the Scottish Sheriff Court. It took six years to reach any conclusions and when the Parliamentary Bill was introduced in 1904 it failed to pass. It eventually passed at its third attempt in 1907. The Royal Commissions on the Poor Laws and Relief of Distress which reported in 1909 dealt with Scotland in a separate report and made separate recommendations. Yet, to the distress of Scottish members, it soon became apparent that the government had little time or inclination to pass a separate Scottish Poor Law Reform Act. Other bills which were presented on finance and estimates of Scottish expenditure were often unscrutinised and legal reforms were often inappropriate to Scottish circumstances.[19]

Imperial federation was seen by its supporters not only as a way to solve the problem of parliamentary congestion, it would also strengthen the unity of the British Empire and claims to the contrary were vigorously denied. It was even successful in attracting Tory adherents such as F.S. Oliver who argued that it should become the blueprint for the future government of the Empire.[20] It was claimed that imperial federation would provide the necessary cohesive bond to maintain loyalty to the increasingly diffuse and abstract ideal of the British imperial mission:

They (the imperial federationists) want to utilise the gigantic strength, moral and material, of the Empire. They see that those great potential forces will waste themselves in isolated effort, however well intentioned, unless they can be focused, concentrated and made operative by Union .... In an empire such as our, centrifugal forces act powerfully and must be counteracted if the Empire is to hold together and grow in consolidated strength. Under the influence of climactic and other natural causes, racial characteristics tend to vary from the common stock. As communities expand, the sense of individuality, of devotion to the community, increases at the inevitable expense of the devotion to the United Kingdom. Fortunately, a strong counteracting force of coherence exists in the sense of loyalty to a grand idea - the Empire - and it must be encouraged.[21]

Scottish supporters of 'home rule all round', as imperial federation was sometimes called, stressed their devotion to the imperial ideal. Home rule would bond the 'British peoples', which included the white Dominion settler colonies, more effectively together. Furthermore, the exclusion of legislation dealing with purely local affairs would allow the Imperial parliament at Westminster to devote more attention to the more serious matters of state. As such, 'home rule all round' fitted in neatly with the growing chorus of politicians and intellectuals who were promoting 'national efficiency'.[22]   So, far from presenting a challenge to the British imperial ethos, Scottish home rule was founded on the premise that it would strengthen and maintain the unity of the British Empire. According to one home ruler, writing in 1888, he had the best interests of the Empire at heart because 'those who advocate such a policy (Scottish home rule) are the true 'Unionists' while those who oppose it are really 'separatists'.'[23] Furthermore, by emphasising that home rule was to be spread throughout the mother and dominion nations of the Empire, Ireland's claim to priority treatment could be diminished.[24]

Scottish home rule was pushed, often it must be said in a half hearted manner, by the Liberal Party. Given that most members of the Scottish Home Rule Association were also Liberal Party members it was not unnatural to find that the party gave official endorsement to this policy at its annual conference in 1888:

> This National Conference is of the opinion that Home Rule should be granted to Scotland, so that the Scottish people could have the sole control and management of their own National Affairs and suggests that the true solution of the question may be found in granting home rule legislatures on a Federal basis to Scotland, England, Ireland and Wales: but in respect to the urgency of the claim of Ireland, declares that this country must have first consideration.[25]

The primacy of Ireland, as we have seen, was not accepted without a fight and brought the rank and file into conflict with the leadership, in particular Rosebery and Morley. The former was suspicious of home rule in general and the latter believed in the primacy of Ireland's case. Both distrusted the Scottish Home Rule Association which they regarded as another of the self-righteous, single issue groups that was deflecting the Liberal Party from its principal objectives and had turned a once unified movement into a collection of squabbling and competing factions.[26] This was especially the case when in 1892 the Scottish Home Rule Association sought to make their cause a test case in the Scottish constituencies. This was seen as undue meddling in the internal politics of the Liberal Party and as far as the leadership was concerned Irish home rule was a priority and Scottish home rule would have to wait its turn. In spite of the leadership's luke warm endorsement, a body of Scottish MPs pushed ahead with the project. The key protagonists were G. B. Clark, William Hunter and Sir Henry Dalziel.

Between 1886 and 1900 seven Scottish home rule motions and federal home rule motions which included Scotland were presented to parliament; in 1889, 1890, 1891, 1892, 1893, 1894 and 1895. On those motions which came to a vote, a majority of Scottish MPs voted in favour except in the first one of 1889: 19 for 22 against. The voting figures for the others were; 1890, 25 for, 17 against, 1891, counted out, 1892, 14 for, 10 against, 1893, 37 for, 22 against, 1894, 35 for 21 against, and 1895, 29 for, 15 against.[27] The 1894 and 1895 motions were carried by a majority in the House, although nothing came of them due to a lack of parliamentary time and the fact that the Liberal Party was defeated in the 1895 and 1900 general elections. The Liberals did badly in Scotland dropping from 45 to 39 MPs in 1895 and from 39 to 34 MPs in 1900. The advent of Conservative governments from 1895 to 1905, which were hostile to home rule, meant that activity was temporarily suspended as the Liberal Party concentrated on its opposition duties and rebuilding itself. Hence, it is only after the general election of 1906 which returned a Liberal government and an overwhelming majority of Liberal MPs in Scotland that the issue began to take off again. What the voting figures in the House of Commons show, however, is that in the period from 1880 to

1895, home rule was building up momentum in terms of the number of times that it was presented to parliament and in the voting strength that it attracted. The fact that more members came to vote on the issue after 1892 shows that the issue was considered to be important. Although figures were down in 1895 (it was before the general election), this can be explained by the fact that it was a Federal motion and was not specific to Scotland. The opposition remained fairly consistent and reflected a unified Conservative and Liberal Unionist hostility to Scottish home rule. However, what the figures also show is that a significant section of the Scottish Liberal Party was not voting for home rule and that these included some senior figures in the party; a fact which caused no end of displeasure among the Association's activists.

Scottish Liberal MPs voted for Scottish home rule for a number of reasons. The one common factor which pervaded their thought, however, was the fact that Scotland was not being governed properly. Scottish home rule was tied in with an on going process of reform which was designed to modify the existing system of government. Consequently, politicians often used home rule and devolution as interchangeable terms when in fact they meant administrative reform. For example, Lord Rosebery claimed that: 'The more I see of our political system, the more I am convinced of this, that in a large measure of devolution, subject always to imperial control, lies the secret of the future working of our Empire.'[28] Numerous measure were taken to make Scottish government more effective. The office of Secretary of Scotland was revived in 1885, and the Scottish Office was created to accompany the new post, although it was set up in London. The various Scottish boards were gradually brought under the control of the Scottish Office and this streamlined the government's Scottish activities. The Private Legislation Procedure (Scotland) Act of 1899 allowed the sitting of commissions in Scotland to consider and suggest legislation for Scotland, which freed it from the London circuit. In 1894 a Scottish Standing Committee was created, only to be dropped by the Conservatives the following year, but revived by the Liberals in 1907, which had the remit of considering and debating all Scottish legislation. Such developments were designed to make the government of Scotland more efficient by devolving more of the decisions to

Scottish parliamentarians. The home rule debate was part of his process. It was only one of a number of possible options for the improvement of government in Scotland.

The vagueness of the home rule proposals was a considerable handicap against the issue making progress and its tendency to become confused with administrative devolution did not help matters either. The early motions called for some form of self-government but were not fleshed out with any detail. The main objective was to establish the validity of the principle. Because of this lack of substance, little interest could be generated outside the Scottish members. By 1895 Dalziel had moved for a Scottish legislature which would deal with the domestic needs of the country. The bill was an easy target for the opposition who claimed that it would lead to the break-up of the Empire and a lessening of the valuable commercial ties with England. In any case, it was claimed that the Scottish home rulers had neither popular support nor a mandate from the Scottish people to present such claims. Enthusiasm from the official Liberal leadership was lacking and the general election in 1895 returned the Conservatives which put paid to the prospect for the meantime. The Scottish Home Rule Association faded into the political wilderness and its leaders gravitated towards the eccentric fringes of Scottish nationalism.

The Rise of Progressivism

Most historians have tended to under-estimate the importance of Scottish home rule in the Edwardian era.[29] It has been seen as an uninteresting by-product of the Irish issue, taken on board by the Liberal leadership to make Irish home rule more palatable to the Scottish electorate. As Henry Dalziel explained to the House of Commons:

> We believe that the more the Irish demand is presented to the country as part of a general settlement on lines applicable to other portions of the United Kingdom, the stronger will be the support given by the British electors to the Irish appeal.[30]

Scottish home rule has also been interpreted as a tactical diversion to delay the passage of the Irish bill by bogging it down into wider constitutional reform for the rest of the United Kingdom.[31] While the previous section of this chapter would endorse the view that Scottish home rule was of marginal significance in the period from 1880 to 1910, the fact is that after this date, the issue came seriously close to dominating Scottish politics before the outbreak of war in 1914.

Central to this development were the activities of the Young Scots Society (YSS) which was formed in 1900 following the crushing Liberal defeat in the general election of that year. The society was formed to educate 'young men in the fundamental principles of Liberalism and stimulating them in the study of social sciences and economics.'[32] The atmosphere of jingoism which had accompanied the general election had exposed the complacency surrounding Liberal Party attitudes regarding the Scottish electorate. The belief that Scotland was insulated from the baser elements of jingoism and that Scottish political behaviour was motivated by lofty idealism was shattered. The impetus for the organisation came after an advert had been placed in the *Edinburgh Evening News* and the Society was formally launched on the 8th of November 1900. The organisation soon attracted publicity. A meeting held on the 26th of April 1901 on South African affairs by the pro-Boer, John Merriman, caused a considerable outcry and disturbance. The organiser, J.M. Hogge, was unrepentant and described the meeting as a 'splendid vindication of the right of free speech'.[33] Even at this early stage in its development, it was apparent that the Young Scots Society was to the left of the mainstream Liberal Party.

The Young Scots got their first political break in 1903 as a result of Joseph Chamberlain's protectionist campaign. The threat to free trade was the ideal panacea for Liberal divisions and was capable of uniting the various factions within the Liberal Party in its defence. In the Autumn of 1903 the Young Scots began their free trade campaign which addressed over 60,000 people and distributed over a million leaflets. The heavy guns of the Liberal Party, such as Leonard McCourtney and Winston Churchill, were brought north to increase the fire power of the campaign. Great play was made of working-class fears that protectionism would increase the price of food and this was neatly encapsulated in the slogan 'Big Loaf or Little Loaf'. Few had any doubts as to the success of the campaign as the following report illustrates:

> One could not but be materially impressed by the hostility of the working man to Mr Chamberlain's proposals. Throughout our long tour, on only one occasion was an amendment moved.... Our tour took us through the enemy's country (we purposely chose Tory counties) and we are strongly convinced that if candidates could be secured who could arouse the industrial portions of the constituencies there would be no doubt that the Liberal could even sweep the Tory west.[34]

Such optimism proved to be well founded with the Liberal Party winning every by election in a vacated Tory seat in Scotland before the general election in 1906. The Society's activities were showered with accolades from the Liberal Party leadership. According to William Harcourt: 'I have followed with satisfaction its (the YSS) vigorous action in reviving and enforcing sound liberal principles in Scotland. It has done much to restore the balance in favour of the Liberal Party, of which we have had such happy experiences lately'.[35] The Young Scots brought a youthful dynamism to the Liberal Party in Scotland and the experience of the free trade campaign was important in sharpening up electoral strategy and tactics.

The Young Scots set themselves the task of reinvigorating the Liberal Party organisation which was believed to be in a run-down condition. The Society formed its organisational network and by 1903, it had over three thousand members in thirty branches. Membership increased throughout the Edwardian period and there may have been as many as ten thousand members in fifty branches by 1914. The Young Scots were not simply content with their own reforms and Liberal Party constituency caucuses were harangued into action:

> 'The Young Scots Society condemns the liberals in West Edinburgh for not pulling their weight. (We) have done a considerable power of work in the constituency, theoretically in conjunction with the Liberals, but practically without their aid or

support. They are conspicuous by their absence at meetings... It is nothing less than a disgrace.[136]

The YSS was determined that the style of campaigning had to change and that there would have to be greater commitment, enthusiasm and hard work in order to win 'Scotland for Liberalism'. The quality of Liberal candidates was found to be wanting and the Young Scots decided to remedy this by, wherever possible, securing the selection of one of their own number: 'We must influence the selection of candidates and get rid of the present haphazard and helpless political nonentities who pose as Scottish candidates.'[137] By 1905, fifteen Young Scots had been placed as parliamentary candidates and the Society had the support of sixteen MPs.[38]

Such organisational endeavours paid off dividends in the 1906 general election which the Liberals won by a landslide in both Scotland and the rest of the United Kingdom. While many acknowledged the work of the Young Scots in highlighting the dangers of the Conservative Party's policy of protectionism, Liberal success was not based on free trade alone. Although the 1906 Liberal government embarked on a series of social reforms, few historians believe that this was a significant factor in shaping the result of the election in England. Party literature south of the border made little reference to social policy and there was little political debate on the issue.[39] This was not the case in Scotland. The *Edinburgh Evening News* and the *Scottish Review* in their election specials stated that social reform would dominate the contest. Other newspapers such as the *Glasgow Herald* and the *Scotsman* likewise gave extensive coverage to social questions. Many radicals had been actively pressing social reform as the main tenet of the new Liberal political philosophy: 'In view of the general election, we are, as a party, preparing to appeal to the country on a programme of social reform. This is as it should be.'[40] A casual survey of Young Scot literature reveals that the organisation put a premium on social issues:

So has Scotland been grievously neglected. All this portrays on the part of the government a contempt for Scottish needs and Scottish opinion which Scotsmen ought to resent and remember

when the general election brings an opportunity for retaliation ...
When the Liberal government arrives, a new spirit must prevail.
New Scottish legislation is sorely needed on such subjects as
education, land, liquor, Church and state, on which we have our
own systems totally different from those of England. On these
questions, Scottish opinion is far ahead of England, and we must
insist that they be treated on their own merits and that our bills
shall not be emasculated to produce an apparent symmetry with
Southern measures.[41]

The 'new' liberalism was enthusiastically embraced north of the border
because it would secure the party's electoral support among the
working class and would see off any potential challenge from the
Labour Party:

> The fact is that old liberalism is doomed. It is in vain that the
> fossils and doctrinaires connected with the party protest against
> the advance of socialism. They have stultified themselves by their
> acquiescence in Irish legislation and the Scottish Crofters Act.
> The conditions that justified these measures for the country
> would equally excuse similar interference with the social
> circumstances of our cities. One sees with regret the riven ranks
> of the progressive party, but the breach can only be healed by a
> frank acceptance of these responsibilities on the part of
> liberalism.... One can seldom give more than a modified
> adhesion to any principle. It is one thing, however, to admit that
> socialism is only capable of a limited application, and quite
> another to condemn, as certain Liberals do, the principle itself -
> to recognise the political and ignore the social problem. If this
> policy persists, one may with perfect confidence predict the
> imminent revolt from Liberalism of the working classes... I look
> to the Young Scots to guide the party in the more excellent way
> of what has been called the New Liberalism. A country resting on
> a starved and ignorant proletariat must inevitably confess its
> impotency and become a despotism... it is among the elect of our
> working class and those in intimate relationship with them that
> we can still happily find the brawn and heart of our nation.[42]

Election literature reflected this concern with social problems and the espousal of progressivism or the new liberalism, together with trumpeting the baleful effects of protectionism, effectively ensured the Liberal Party the support of the working-class and the electoral dominance of Scotland in 1906.[43]

The 1906 election set the benchmark for the subsequent development of pre-1914 Scottish politics. The Conservatives and Liberal Unionists were awe struck by the totality of their defeat and set to work emulating the activities of the Young Scots by setting up their own organisation, the Junior Imperial League, without much success.[44] The radical edge of Scottish liberalism was reinforced by electoral success and the intake of new Young Scots MPs. Debates about social reform continued and occupied the core of organisational activity and a substantial literary output. Radical demands were further fuelled by the persistent meddling of the Conservative dominated House of Lords with Liberal legislation and a lack of parliamentary time. For an increasing number within the ranks of the YSS, the solution to these two problems was reform of the House of Lords and the creation of a Scottish parliament:

taking into consideration that at the general election (1906), Scotland by an overwhelming vote, expressed her desire for certain measures of long delayed reform by returning five sixths of her entire representation in Parliament to support the government, that the legislation desired, not having been effected, resolved, in view of the congestion of business in parliament, and of the intolerable attitude of the House of Lords towards government proposals, that the time has arrived for the organisation of a national movement in favour of self-government and the supremacy of the House of Commons.[45]

Scottish nationalism with a small 'n' had always been part and parcel of the Scottish radical tradition and Liberal MPs had been putting forward Scottish home rule bills in Parliament from the 1890s. As we have seen most of these bills had been adjuncts to Irish home rule and had little thought or momentum behind them. Scottish parliamentarians in the

Edwardian era, however, began to look to home rule as a pragmatic device to implement social policy and reform. Unlike the late Victorian period when a Scottish parliament was mooted as a good thing in itself, radical Liberals now came to view it as a means to an end. It was a device which would effectively deliver the policies which occupied a high priority on the political agenda.

A Scottish parliament only became a serious policy option when the issue of social reform gained wider political currency. This happened for four reasons. Firstly, there was the practical difficulty of legislating specific reform for Scotland. According to the MP for Aberdeen North, D.V. Pirie, the social issues of temperance, education and land reform had to be framed to fit the Scottish legal system and the six hours of parliamentary time allocated to Scottish legislation was unable to do justice to these complex issues.[46] Secondly, the Scots had already seen the important reforms such as the 1908 Children's Act mangled and deformed to fit Scottish law because of a lack of parliamentary time which raised serious questions as to the ability of Westminster to deliver appropriate and specific Scottish legislation. Thirdly, many Scottish Liberals believed that the social reform in Scotland was being delayed by English conservatism. Time and time again it was claimed that 'there is not one single item in the whole programme of Radicalism or social reform today, which, if Scotland had powers to pass laws, would not have been carried out a quarter of a century ago.'[47] Finally, given that social reform was the core radical objective and that the Westminster parliament was believed to be ineffective in realising such aspirations, the obvious conclusion for many was to create a Scottish parliament that would deal with domestic legislation. It was with this prospect in mind that the Liberal Party Conference passed a motion to set up a National Committee with the specific remit of formulating strategy on home rule.[48]

The January and December general elections of 1910 in Scotland were fought on predominantly British issues, the first on reform of the House of Lords and the second on Irish home rule. It was accepted by most Liberals that progress on home rule would not be possible until the stumbling block of the House of Lords was removed. The Liberals consolidated and marginally improved their position in Scotland by winning an extra seat from the Unionists which was in contradistinction to the situation in England where the Conservatives recovered their position leaving the two parties almost equal. The Liberals were only able to continue in government due to the support of the Irish Nationalists. Undoubtedly the party machine played a major part in the Liberal success north of the border. The same aggressive campaigning techniques which had brought success in 1906 were used to good effect in 1910. Marginal seats were targeted, speaking tours arranged, open air demonstrations against the House of Lords were held and over a million propaganda leaflets were distributed.[49] Even the Conservatives were forced to admit that they were powerless in the face of the 'radical machine'.[50]

For the radicals, the House of Lord's obstruction of social and land reform formed the crux of the campaign. Vehement class rhetoric was used against the unelected and idle rich who opposed the will of the people. [51] The Liberals were able to capitalise on a century's worth of Scottish resentment against the landowning class who were pilloried for their 'unearned income', causing evictions and emigration, and their unjust and undemocratic use of patronage. The Conservative and Unionist camp, on the other hand, conducted a rather lack lustre campaign focusing on the danger to property from the 'People's' Budget', imperial defence, protection against local vetoes on the drink trade and vague promises were made on holding a referendum before tariff reform was introduced.[52] In essence, there was little to distinguish it from the campaign south of the border. The reform of the House of Lords after the Parliament Bill, however, not only opened up the possibility of more social legislation, it also removed the most reliable brake on Irish home rule and this prospect galvanised the Unionist camp into action in the December election of 1910. '80 Irish votes, the price of home rule' thundered the Liberal Unionist manifesto which accused the Asquith government of bartering British unity and security for the support of the 'Irish revolutionary party'. Appeals were made to loyal Protestants not to forsake their fellow countrymen in Ulster and 'fight as never before for the maintenance of the Union'. [53] British patriotism formed the main component of the Conservative and Liberal Unionist campaign and it was hoped that this would pay electoral dividends. It did not. Although the Unionist vote went up marginally from 39.6 to 42.6%, both parties failed to take any more seats. The

Liberals continued with the same themes of the earlier campaign, although Scottish home rule was promoted higher up the agenda by the radicals. [54] The December election was fought by all sides in a spirit of exhaustion and the turn out was lower than January.[55]

In the period from 1910 to the eve of the First World War, Scottish politics was dominated by Irish and Scottish home rule. The radicals made Scottish home rule their priority:

> Victory for the Commons now being assured, the Young Scots society returns to its home rule propaganda, and intends to push the issue with all the energy it can command. Devolution is after the abolition of the House of Lords veto, the most urgent reform of the time.[56]

It was formally adopted as part of the Young Scots constitution and it was held to be the key to all further social reform:

> We submit to the government that they make home rule for Scotland, as a means to land reform and general social reform on national lines, the supreme issue of the Scottish policy ... We urge all Scottish progressive members to cease to cherish vain hopes of Scottish reform from London.[57]

Campaigns were undertaken to promote the cause through out the country, with over three hundred meetings held in 1911. Publications were churned out by the thousand. Ten thousand copies of the *Young Scot Handbook*, fifty thousand copies of *Home Rule: the Case in 60 points* and tens of thousands of leaflets were published.[58]

Young Scots began to take a harder line on the issue and increasingly began to meddle in the internal politics of the Liberal Party to promote greater discipline and advocated the setting up of a 'Nationalist' group of Scottish MPs:

> A pledge from every candidate for a Scottish constituency to insist upon the granting of Scottish home rule must now be secure. Only by the formation of a strong Scottish nationalist

party can Scotland hope to secure adequate recognition of her needs.[59]

The Young Scots badgered sitting Liberal MPs and examined their record on support for a Scottish parliament. English 'invaders' who had safe seats in Scotland were monitored and those who were absent from the 1912 Scottish home rule bill parliamentary division were made to account for themselves: 'I had thought of dealing with those gentlemen not in their places to assist us, but I find that a number of them are ill and only Churchill and Falconer remain to be dealt with.'[60] Furthermore, the Young Scots were also screening prospective Liberal candidates and nominations from English candidates for Scottish seats were blocked. If such demands were not met, the YSS threatened to run its own candidates and use its organisational and campaigning power against the Liberal Party:

> The Society (demands) Scottish home rule during the present parliament and pledging itself, if necessary, to enforce this demand by running its own candidates. The threatened adoption of Mr Scaramanga Ralli as the Liberal candidate at the Ross and Cromarty by election in June and the actual adoption of Mr Masterman by the Liberals in the Tradeston by-election in July, almost led YSS candidatures to enforce the spirit of this resolution, because these gentlemen, by inevitable lack of sympathy with the Scottish national point of view, would have been a hindrance to the national movement. Mr MacPherson just secured the nomination in the former case, and in the later, Mr Masterman, after accepting promptly made way for Dr Dundas White.[61]

While it is not clear that the YSS really intended to carry out such threats to the letter, the fact that the Liberal Party saw fit not to challenge the Society is clear evidence of the influence the organisation enjoyed. Given the role the YSS played in the Liberal Party's electoral machine and the fact that a good number of Liberal MPs depended on the organisation for support at election times, it would have been a risky business to antagonise them. Furthermore, the Society had been fairly open in its assessment of the respective merits of prospective Liberal candidates and their attitudes to home rule. As early as April 1905, the Labour candidate for Blackfriars in Glasgow was promoted as a better prospect for progressivism than the Liberal.[62] Also, the Society began to take steps to formally distance itself from the Liberal Party and objections were raised in 1912 to the fact that the YSS appeared in the *Liberal Handbook* as a 'party organisation'.[63] Some radicals expressed disquiet that in by elections after 1910 the YSS always gave its support to the Liberal Party even though Labour candidates were more sound on 'progressive principles'.[64] Many Young Scots were determined that the Liberal leadership could not take the Society's support for granted.

All this gave the issue an unprecedented momentum which even the Conservative and Unionist Party was forced to acknowledge:

> It is believed that, in varying degrees, in most Scottish constituencies, Unionist candidates and workers will be met with the question of Scottish home rule by way of heckling in platform work and canvassing. Every radical (Liberal) member and candidate is more or less pledged to Scottish home rule, many of them directly and emphatically, and the machine driven radical associations throughout Scotland, officially at least, are eager in its support and if the radicals are returned at a general election they would declare that they had a mandate for home rule.[65]

This confidential communiqué was issue in 1914 to prospective candidates in anticipation of the general election which should have occurred in 1915. As we shall see, Unionists persistently played down the existence of popular support for Scottish home rule in public. Yet, this private memorandum is clear evidence of how seriously the issue was taken and is a tacit admission that the political tide had turned in favour of home rule after 1910. It was an eloquent testament to the endeavours of the Young Scots.

Notions that Scottish home rule was simply promoted in order to make Irish home rule more palatable to the Scottish electorate and/or act as a delaying tactic is not borne out by the evidence. Firstly, it was often claimed that home rule, both Irish and Scottish, was supported to please Catholic Irish constituents in Scotland. The Unionist H.J. Mackinder claimed that the Liberal Party in Scotland was dependent on the Irish vote and that 'There are not a few hon. gentlemen opposite- I am not quite certain that it is not the majority of them - who hold their seat by virtue of Irish sentiment in Scotland and not Scottish sentiment at all.' [66] This proposition does not cut much ice, then and now because the vast majority of the Irish Catholic constituency did not have the vote. Before the Reform Act of 1918, about forty per cent of all adult males did not have the franchise and this penalised working-class men at the lower level of the socio-economic spectrum, where most of the Irish Catholic community were to be found. In any case, the most vociferous supporters of Irish home rule in Scotland represented constituencies with little or no Catholic population, the one exception being Dundee. John Morley represented East Fife, and D.V. Pirie represented Aberdeen, for example. Secondly, too much attention has focused on the Churchill's Dundee speech of 1911 in which he propounded a scheme of devolution for the whole of the United Kingdom including the regions of England.[67] As has hopefully been demonstrated, the home rule campaign in Scotland was well underway in Scotland before this time. Churchill did not create support for home rule all round in Scotland, rather he was reacting to a ground swell of opinion that already existed. While Churchill's endorsement may have been fuelled by political expediency, there is no reason to tar the activities of many Liberal MPs and rank and file activists with the same brush.

A final argument can be used to show that Scottish home rule had an independent dynamic separate from Irish home rule. Scottish home rulers remained ambivalent in their attitudes towards Ireland and, indeed, muted threats were made to block Irish home rule if it was passed on its own and not as part of a wider devolutionary package: 'To attempt the grant of Home Rule to Ireland without regard to the necessities of other nations is to court disaster.'[68] The principal argument used by Scottish parliamentarians in favour of home rule was that it should be part of a package of imperial reform which would promote 'national efficiency': 'The disentanglement of all local and national transactions from imperial affairs would liberate and strengthen the Parliament for imperial concerns.'[69] Indeed, Sir Henry

Cowan claimed that the issue was an 'imperial question' and a valuable contribution to the 'solution of the problem of congestion at parliament.'[70] Up until the Irish Home Rule Bill was passed in 1912, Scottish parliamentarians expected that Scotland would be included in the first wave of devolutionary legislation. Indeed, one of the key reasons why the Young Scots began to exert pressure on the Liberal Party after 1911 was the expectation that Scottish home rule would be on the statute book along with Irish home rule within the lifetime of the current parliament.[71] As one parliamentarian put it: 'If a similar measure of self-government is denied to Scotland, such a wave of indignation will spread over that country as will shake every Liberal seat to its foundation.'[72] Scottish home rulers wanted to tie Irish and Scottish legislation together because a British parliament with reduced Irish representation would make it more difficult for the Scots to attain their own objective as it was believed that this would leave them at the mercy of an increased English majority in parliament. Although the Irish bill went through first, Sir Henry Cowan's Scottish Bill passed its second reading on 30 May 1913 and looked set to reach the statute book.

The cause of Scottish home rule did not have an easy parliamentary passage. Firstly, the period from 1910 to 1914 was one of recurring crises in British politics and the Liberal government had more than enough on its plate without diverting too much energy to the problems of the northern kingdom. There was mounting labour unrest, public demonstrations by militant suffragettes, near civil war in Ireland and mounting tensions in foreign policy. From the outset, Scottish home rule would not receive much time in an over-crowded parliamentary timetable. A second difficulty was the sniping campaign mounted by the opposition. The prospect of the disintegration of the United Kingdom was horrific enough to merge the Conservatives and Liberal Unionists into the Unionist Party in 1912. Defence of the Union and the Empire formed the core of the party's political programme. The Unionists sought to exploit the growing divisions within the Scottish Liberal Party. Although the radicals had been instrumental in pushing Scottish home rule and social reform to the fore, this was not to everyone's taste. Tensions between the Liberal Party and the Young Scots became strained and the coercive methods used to ensure compliance, including the threat of running their own candidates or supporting the Labour Party alienated some party officials.[73]:

Unionists claimed that there was no real demand for Scottish home rule and that the impetus came from the Young Scots who were branded as a clique It was pointed out that of forty six Liberal candidates' manifestos in the December 1910 election, only twenty two mentioned either Scottish or Irish home rule.[74] The Unionists accused the Liberal government of being blackmailed by an 'obscure clique' who were using underhand techniques to impose their policies against the democratic wishes of the Scottish people.[75] The threat to property and the financial burden of a Scottish parliament, not to mention the loosening of ties with the Empire, were cast up to appeal to middle class fears:

> Do honourable members opposite think that young Scotchmen, with the world before them, wish to have the doors closed upon them and have the spirit of hostility raised against them on the part of the predominant partner where there are so many openings to career?[76]

The Frontbench's silence on the issue did little to dispel such notions and the fact that many of them sat for Scottish seats reinforced Unionist suspicions. Furthermore, banging the Unionist drum appeared to be paying dividends as the party's by-election performances started to show signs of improvement. Unionists promoted the imperialist vision of Scottish identity in response to the demands for home rule and party workers were urged to: 'take up a positive and if need be aggressive policy and point to the importance which Scottish national patriotism has played and still must play in the wider patriotism of the British Empire.'[77]   As with the Liberals, the Unionist argued that Scotland's position within the Empire had to be maintained and reinforced. Whereas the Liberals argued that home rule would improve 'national efficiency' by making the Westminster parliament more effective, the Unionists claimed that it would lessen the imperial ties which all regarded as so important to Scottish well-being:

To revive in Scotland or Ireland National Legislators (sic) is to debase and degrade both these countries from the fine position they now hold as equal partners in the imperial government and make them tenth rate, wretched, one horse tributary states.[78]

Unionists promoted fears that the Scots were in danger of raising old animosities which had been buried in 1707 and risked losing the status and power that they now enjoyed as part of the world's foremost imperial power. The Marquis of Tulibardine claimed that home rule would put the nation back 'into the small backwater of Scotland and into the separation in which we were before the Union.'[79] The prosperity and progress of post Union Scotland was contrasted with the poverty and backwardness of the pre-union era, and it was assumed by the Unionists that home rule would inevitably lead to the latter. In any case, it was argued that the Union did not threaten Scottish identity, on the contrary it strengthened it. According to Andrew Bonar Law, the leader of the Unionist Party:

There is no one who will deny that Scotch character or Scotch nationality is as firmly rooted as that of any people in the world, and that after two centuries of the closest of connections with England. It proves beyond a shadow of a doubt that whatever is good in nationality can continue and even increase, in spite of union with a larger country.[80]

In short, the benefits of Union far outweighed the changes associated with change.

In spite of the passions generated, it all came to nothing. The outbreak of war in August 1914 suspended home rule for the meantime. In its initial stages, the war induced a remarkable sense of unity. Liberals and Unionist forgot about their petty differences over home rule, and instead, concentrated on the danger to British security. In spite of the fact that the Young Scots had been formed in 1900 as a reaction to the threat of jingoism generated by the Boer War, most members rushed to condemn German militarism and support the government. Yet, the facade of unity did not last long. Radicals gravitated towards the Labour Party which was the up and coming force in Scottish politics. The Liberal Party, which seemed in 1914 to be unassailable, split apart and began a process of slow disintegration. The Unionists, who had lost three election in a row and who believed that their power and influence was set to diminish further, found that the war rejuvinated their fortunes. The seeds of home rule which had been planted before 1914 needed to be hardy enough to withstand the onslaught of total war and the climactic changes which followed in its wake.

NOTES

[1] See D.G. Boyce, *The Irish Question and British politics, 1868-1996,* (London, 1996).

[2] Quoted R.R. James, *Rosebery: A Biography of Archibald Philip, 5th Earl of Rosebery,* (London, 1963), p. 130.

[3] *Scotsman,* 27 Sep. 1871.

[4] R.Colls and P. Dodds (ed), *Englishness: Political and Cultural,* (London, 1986).

[5] William A. Hunter, *The Financial Relations of England and Scotland,* (Edinburgh, 1892).

[6] *Ibid.*

[7] Lady Frances Balfour, *Lord Balfour of Burleigh,* (London, 1924), pp. 89-95.

[8] I.G.C. Hutchison, *A Political History of Modern Scotland, 1832-1924: Parties, Elections and Issues,* (Edinburgh, 1986), pp. 171-3.

[9] John Downie, 'How the Scottish Union has Worked', *Scottish Review,* Oct. 1892.

[10] H.J. Hanham, 'The Creation of the Scottish Office, 1881-87', *Juridical Review,* 10 (1965), pp. 205-36 and Convention of Royal Burghs of Scotland, *The National Meeting in Scotland in Favour of the Creation of a Separate Department of State for Scotland,* (Edinburgh, 1900).

[11] Hunter, *Financial Relations.*

[12] *Protest of the Scottish Home Rule Association Against the Denial or Delay of Scottish Home Rule,* (Edinburgh, 1890).

[13] William Mitchell, *The Political Situation in Scotland,* (Edinburgh, 1893).

[14] Scottish Home Rule Association, *The Union of 1707 Viewed Financially,* (Edinburgh, 1888), p. 2.

[15] This emerges in nationalist periodicals such as *The Scottish Nationalist*.

[16] Quoted H.J. Hanham, *Scottish Nationalism,* (London, 1969), p. 120.

[17] *Scotsman*, 2 Dec. 1886, speech of John Morley in Edinburgh.

[18] William Mitchell, *Home Rule for Scotland and Imperial Federation,* (Edinburgh, 1892).

[19] For a catalogue of the failings of the parliamentary system see Walter Murray, *Scottish Home Rule: The Case in 60 Points*, (Glasgow, 1912).

[20] John Kendle, "The Round Table Movement and Home Rule All Round', *Historical Journal*, 11 (1968), pp. 332-53.

[21] The Earl of Dunraven, 'The Future of Ireland, Settlement by Consent', *Nineteenth Century*, 63 (1913), pp. 208-9.

[22] Scottish Home Rule Association, *The Evils of Centralisation and its Cure,* (Edinburgh, 1898).

[23] *Scottish Review*, April 1888, p. 40.

[24] T.D. Wanliss, *Bars to British Unity or a Plea for National Sentiment,* (Edinburgh, 1895).

[25] University of Edinburgh, Minutes of the Scottish Liberal Association, 1888.

[26] Hanham, *Scottish Nationalism,* p. 92.

[27] Information taken from *H.C. Debs.*

[28] *Scotsman*, Jan. 18 1895.

[29] P. Jalland, 'United Kingdom Devolution, 1910-14: Political Panacea or Tactical Diversion', *English Historical Review*, 94 (1979), pp. 757-85.

[30] *H.C. Debs.* vol. XXIX, col. 1930, 16 August 1911.

[31] Jalland, 'United Kingdom Devolution'.

[32] Young Scots Prospectus, 1903.

[33] *Edinburgh Evening News*, 27 April 1901.

[34] *Young Scot*, 1 Oct. 1903, p.7..

[35] NLS, Acc. 3721, Box 140, William Harcourt to General Secretary John Gulland, 2 May 1904.

[36] *ibid.,* 1 Dec. 1904, p. 26.

[37] *ibid.*

[38] This information is taken from the Society's journal, *the Young Scot*. Although some MPs gave only nominal support, their presence was significant nonetheless. The MPs were; Campbell-Bannerman; D.V. Pirie; James Bryce; J.S. Ainsworth; A.W. Black; R.T. Reid; George MacRae; John D. Hope; The Master of Elibank; Thomas Shaw; John A. Dewar; Dr Rarquharson; J.W. Crombie; J.H. Dalziel; Alexander Ure and T.R. Buchanan. Prospective candidates were; Arthur Dewar; C.E. Price; J.A.

Murray MacDonald; Norman Lamont; Sir John Jardine; D.M. Smeaton; Leonard Courtney; Joseph Dobbie; D. Laidlaw; J.M. Hogge; Robert Munro; D.J. Downie; H. Watt and Robert Hay.

[39] See G.R.Searle, *The Liberal Party: Triumph and Disintegration, 1886-1929*, (London, 1992), pp. 79-81.

[40] *Young Scot,* 1 May 1905, p. 92.

[41] NLS, Acc. 3721, Box 140, Young Scot prospectus, 1904.

[42] *Young Scot.,* 1 May 1905, p. 94.

[43] NLS, Acc 3721, Box 146, 'Election Literature'.

[44] Hutchison, *Political History,* p.223.

[45] NLS, Acc. 3721, Box 146, 'Parliamentary Committee 1907-1911', YSS Annual Conference Report, 6 April 1907.

[46] *H.C. Debs.*, vol CLXX IX, 26 May 1908, p. 967.

[47] *ibid.,* 16 August 1911, col. 1929-30.

[48] *Glasgow Herald*, 30 June 1910.

[49] NLS, Acc. 3721, Box 146, 'Report of the Publications Committee'.

[50] NLS, Conservative Party Mss., *Younger Memorandum,* 1914, p.3.

[51] For example, see press reports of the open air demonstration on 3 September and the speaking tour from 31 October to 4 November 1910.

[52] Taken from press reports of the campaign, *Glasgow Herald,* October 1910.

[53] Liberal Unionist Manifesto, reprinted in *Glasgow Herald,* 29 December 1909.

[54] *Young Scots Handbook 1911.*

[55] Hutchison, *Political History,* pp. 218-21.

[56] *Young Scots Handbook 1911*

[57] NLS, Acc. 3721, box 146/2, Young Scots Society, *Report of the Annual Conference, 1911.*

[58] *ibid.,* 'Publication Committee 1912'.

[59] *Young Scots Handbook 1911,* p. 13

[60] NLS, Acc. 372, Box 144, Thomas Lockhead (Hon. General Secretary YSS, to R.E. Muirhead, 9 March 1912.

[61] *Young Scots Handbook 1911,* p.2.

[62] *Young Scot*, April 1905, p. 81.

[63] NLS, Acc.3721, Box 146, 'Parliamentary Committee', Thomas Lockhead to R.E. Muirhead, 31 Jan. 1912.

[64] *ibid.,* 'National Council', undated resolution c. 1912.

[65] *Younger Memorandum: Scots Home Rule,* 19 May 1914.

[66] *H.C. Debs.*, vol. CLXXX IX, col. 1461, 26 May 1908.

[67] Jalland, 'United Kingdom Devolution'.

[68] *Manifesto and Appeal to the Scottish People on Scottish Home Rule*, July 1911.

[69] Robert Munro Ferguson, *H.C. Debs.*, vol XXXIV, col. 1454, 28 Feb. 1912.

[70] *ibid.*, col. 455.

[71] NLS, Acc. 3721, Box 146, 'Parliamentary Committee'.

[72] *ibid.*, Dr Chapple, col. 1446.

[73] NLS, Acc. 3721, box 146, Thomas Lockhead (General Secretary of the Young Scots Society) to R.E. Muirhead, 9 March 1912. Correspondence between R.E. Muirhead and Walter Murray, September 1911.

[74] *H.C. Debs*, vol XXXIV, 28 February 1912, col. 1466-7

[75] *ibid.*

[76] *ibid.*, vol. XXIX, col. 1936, Sir Henry Craik, 16 Aug. 1911.

[77] *Younger Memorandum.*

[78] NLS, Scottish Home Rule Collection, Lord Lorne to John Romans, 21 Nov. 1889.

[79] *H.D. Debs.*, Vol. XXIV, col. 1466, 28 Feb. 1912.

[80] *ibid.*, col. 1487.

CHAPTER THREE

The Birth of Modern Nationalism and the Search for a Strategy, 1918-1939

At the end of the First World War, Scottish home rulers remained fairly confident of their prospects for success. In spite of the massive social, economic and political changes which the war had brought in its wake, most believed that the issue could be taken up from where it was left in August 1914. Indeed, some were even more confident and used the experiences of the last four years to further justify their case. The war had witnessed greater control from London which was deemed to be inefficient. Inexperienced and distant administrators were out of touch with what was happening in Scotland and the creation of bureaucratic infrastructures simply complicated the effective management of the war effort north of the border. According to one radical Liberal, J.M. Hogge:

> The experience of war, particularly of the control of the various government departments over Scottish business itself, has probably made more converts to a system of Scottish home rule than all the speeches that have ever been made on Scottish platforms; or by decisions we have taken here (in the House of Commons).[1]

The moral climate of the Versailles peace treaty negotiations was favourable to the concept of small nations exercising greater control over their own affairs. Indeed, an appeal to have Scotland represented at the Paris Peace Conference was sent. *La Petition National de l'Ecosse pour obtenir sa Representation au Congress de la Paix,* however, fell on deaf ears. The Labour Party and the Trade Unions had emerged as major players in Scottish politics and, if anything, were even more favourable to home rule than the Liberals. At the annual conference of the STUC in 1918, it was claimed that a Scottish parliament should be set up to avoid 'sending deputations to people in London who know nothing of our wants.'[2] Continuous attempts by the London headquarters to circumvent the autonomy of Scottish Trade Unions , the Scottish Co-operative Movement and local Labour Party branches lead to widespread resentment at outside interference and the endorsement of Scottish self-government was seen as an effective way to guarantee local independence.[3] Also, Scottish home rule had been one of the staple policies of the Labour movement in the pre-war period.[4]

The Second Scottish Home Rule Association

For many, it seemed that the war was simply a temporary disruption and that the pre-war home rule agitation would be easy to pick up. Consequently in 1918, the Scottish Home Rule Association was reformed by Roland Muirhead, a former Young Scot who was a co-founder of the socialist newspaper, *Forward,* and a member of the Independent Labour Party. The SHRA was a very different animal from its cranky and chaotic Victorian predecessor. Muirhead brought organisational skills to the Association and was prepared to help fund it. He was also determined to iron out, as he saw it, the weakness of previous campaigns. Muirhead believed that the cause of Scottish home rule in the Edwardian period had been compromised by too close an association between the Young Scots and the Liberal Party. The post-war SHRA was designed to be non-party and thus have greater freedom of action.[5] However, given the changing nature of the Scottish political landscape, it was expected that the membership of the SHRA could not help but reflect a greater bias towards the Labour movement. The belief that too close a relationship with the Liberal Party in the past had compromised the movement meant that there would be a greater concentration on pressure group tactics. After all, the increasingly uncompromising attitude of the Young Scots after 1910 had paid off dividends and home rule was made a serious political priority. For Muirhead and others, one more push was all that was needed to achieve the Scottish parliament.

The composition of the SHRA soon reflected the dominance of the Labour movement in Scottish post-war radical politics. The Liberals were divided and although far from finished, had begun a long and tortuous process of self-disintegration.[6] The trade unions, with large affiliated memberships, were able to dominate Association policy and the Executive by virtue of having the largest numbers. They were also important in providing funds, organisation and meeting places.[7]

Labour's commitment to home rule in the early twenties was enthusiastic and leading figures such as David Kirkwood and James Maxton were regular performers at SHRA demonstrations which attracted audiences of several thousands.[8] The reasons why the Labour Party should support Scottish home rule were relatively straight forward. As home rule was bound up in the pre-war era with social policy, it should come as no surprise, therefore to find that the party of the working-class should be committed to a parliament in Edinburgh which would help to establish the New Jerusalem north of the border. As James Maxton put it: 'he wanted nothing more than to see aristocratic ridden, English Ridden Scotland turned in to a free Socialist Commonwealth.'[9] Home rule also helped paper over some of the ideological differences in the Scottish Labour Party. At a time when the ideological melting pot had not yet congealed into a coherent package, home rule was one of the few items which had universal approval. It united left wingers such as James Maxton with more moderate souls such as the Rev James Barr. Furthermore, it was popular with the local audiences. Edifying and enlightening as the didactic of Marxism may have been, the message that everything could be blamed on a remote government in England struck a resonant chord among the populace and anti-English jibes were a platform speciality with many of Labour's best speakers.[10]

SHRA optimism was reinforced by the speed at which Labour stormed the electoral barricades. From a modest showing in the general election of 1918, the party emerged as the largest in Scotland with twenty nine seats (and an officially sponsored communist MP) in the election of 1922.[11] The prospect of a Labour Government looked a real possibility and with this came an real opportunity for the enactment of Scottish home rule. It was this possibility which held the Association together. The growth of the SHRA went in tandem with the growth of Labour. By 1920, the Association had over a thousand individual members and 138 organisation gave affiliated support. The SHRA was active in canvassing the view of prospective parliamentary candidates and following the general election of 1922, the Association could notch up forty three MPs who professed support for the home rule cause.[12] Although there had been disquiet at the way in which the Labour Party had regarded the SHRA as a mere appendage of the Labour movement as a whole and had shown great reluctance to tolerate in its ranks those from other parties, it seemed of minor concern given that home rule legislation was likely in the near future. This argument was used by Muirhead who believed that it did not really matter how home rule came about, so long as it was achieved and a Labour government was the most likely method of delivery. [13]

The advent of a minority Labour Government in early 1924, and the opportunity it presented for a Private Members Bill, sponsored by Gorbals MP, George Buchanan, on Scottish home rule, raised many expectations. A large rally was held in April at St Andrews Hall in Glasgow which was enthusiastically supported and well attended.[14] All potential supporters of Scottish home rule in the Commons were contacted and urged to give their support. The SHRA leadership was confident of success, especially as the Prime Minister, Ramsay MacDonald, had been president of the London branch of the Scottish Home Rule Association before the war.[15] Such hopes and expectations were soon dashed, however. The debate, held on 9 May, got off to a bad start. The Scottish Secretary, William Adamson, was lukewarm and showed little obvious enthusiasm. There was little time and the Speaker refused to move the motion to a vote which caused an outburst of complaint and scenes of disruption which further enhanced the Clydesider's reputation for ignorance of the niceties of parliamentary procedure.[16] Endeavours to get the Prime Minister to reschedule a debate and motion proved fruitless, much to the dismay of home rule activists.[17] An attempt to set up a cross party select committee to discuss the issue fell through. MacDonald, it was reported, 'regretted to find that the Conservative party was not prepared to concur in this course, and it could not be carried out. As to the future, he declines to give any pledge'.[18] The optimism of early 1924 soon gave way to pessimism.

The effect of the failure of Buchanan's Bill initiated a reassessment of the strategy employed by the SHRA. A National Convention was established in November 1924 to keep the pressure on parliament.[19] Enthusiasm among the Labour Party was declining as indicated by the fact that only seven MPs turned up to the first meeting.[20] The Parliamentary Committee, which had the remit of drafting a new home rule bill, had made little progress by April 1925 and in the following year, it was bluntly stated that the Labour Party reserved the right to proceed with the issue as they saw best:

> The Sub-committee of the Scottish Labour group think that it is right to point out that ... a future Labour Government will exercise its own judgement as to the lines on which it will frame a bill for the granting of self-government to Scotland.[21]

Muirhead's initial hope that Scottish home rule could escape from the intrigue of party politics was confounded. Attempts by activists in the SHRA to put greater pressure on the Labour Party were curtailed by the trade unions who, by virtue of affiliated membership, held the balance of power in the Association's Executive. Arguments that the SHRA should only endorse candidates which made home rule an immediate priority were dismissed. Labour Party members would not accept any meddling in internal party policy. According to one member, David N. MacKay, the best policy was to wait for another Labour government. As to the priority of home rule, the Association was told that he was a socialist first and a nationalist second.[22] Party political interest emerged triumphant over home rule aspirations and this increasingly effected the conduct of SHRA activity which was largely marginal to Labour's interests. Attendance at meetings and rallies began to fall off and pessimism permeated much of the Association's activities. The effective hijacking of the SHRA and the home rule issue by the Labour Party left the Association little to do other than wait for the next Labour government. William Wright MP wrote to Muirhead in 1925:

> I am renewing my annual subscription to the SHRA with some reluctance. Not because of the amount subscribed, but one feels that the golden moments are passing and little progress is being made. I feel had we met with self-government in Scotland in 1923, we should have accomplished ten times as much work.[23]

Things came to a crunch in May 1927, when the Rev James Barr had the opportunity to introduce a private member's bill on Scottish home rule. The event rekindled some enthusiasm among the activists in the

SHRA and the bill was described as the most thoroughly prepared one to date. Although most would have been surprised had the bill made it on to the statute book, given that Labour was in opposition, few expected that the party would make such a public declaration of indifference on the issue. It was given a half-hearted introduction by Barr and its cosponsor, Thomas Johnston, and after only forty five minutes of debate, it was dropped without a vote. To make matters worse, both later admitted that the bill had been a bad idea.[24]

For many home rule activists in the SHRA, this was the last straw. Frustration had been building up at Labour's apparent lack of enthusiasm and several had warned that if Barr's bill proved to be a failure then 'a more assertive policy is called for'.[25] In October 1927 an organisation within the SHRA called 'the Scottish National Party Group' announced its existence and its intention to undertake independent political action: 'This group was formed to press for the formation of a Scottish National Party - and when funds permit - to fight for every seat, both for parliament and municipal contests'.[26] Acrimony between home rule activists and Labour loyalists in the Scottish National Convention continued and by December 1927, this had turned into outright warfare with accusations being made that Labour MPs had been given instructions 'to do nothing that would imperil the future prospects of the party holding office at Westminster'.[27] As far as many Labour loyalists were concerned, the pressures from home rule activists were interfering with the best interests of the party. According to James Maxton, he would not cooperate with Liberals and Tories to push through home rule at the expense of damaging the prospects for a Labour government.[28] Attempts to promote independent SHRA candidates and a 'national party' were blocked by the trade unions on the Executive.[29] It had become apparent to the home rule activists that the Association was little more than a Labour Party puppet. In January 1928, Muirhead decided to stand as an independent home rule candidate for the constituency of West Renfrewshire. The seat was chosen because the Labour Party had not yet placed a candidate and Muirhead tried to get endorsement from the SHRA Executive. When this was not forthcoming, he quit the Association and in April all like minded activists were urged to follow him into the newly formed National

Party of Scotland.[30] The experience of the SHRA had demonstrated the difficulty of using pressure group tactics on British political parties. Unlike the Edwardian period, party discipline was much tighter in the inter-war years and single issue groups were treated with suspicion. The campaign for a Scottish parliament had to compete against British political priorities, and failed miserably. For home rule activists, there was no other option but to take matters into their own hands.

Nationalism Divided

The National Party of Scotland was formed in April 1928 from members of the Scottish National League, the Scottish National Movement, the Glasgow University Scottish Nationalist Association and disaffected members of the Scottish Home Rule Association.[31] It was a disparate membership and contained a wide spectrum of ideological beliefs. The Scottish National League was made up primarily of 'fundamentalists'; those who believed that the only way to ensure self government in Scotland was to contest elections in order to obtain a mandate from the Scottish people by means of winning a majority of Scottish parliamentary seats. This would form the basis for formal negotiations with Westminster for greater Scottish autonomy. The SNL contained many fundamentalists who tended to be committed to the idea that Scotland should have full political independence from Britain and the Empire.[32] Despite the best efforts of Tom Gibson to move the League towards a more pragmatic and practical stance on Scottish politics, the SNL was heavily associated with ideas of Celtic racialism. Hugh MacDiarmid (C.M. Grieve) and Rhuaridh Erskine of Mar promoted the notion that the Scots needed to rediscover the Celtic racial consciousness and that the nation should look to Ireland for inspiration in the fight against English colonialism.[33] While the group was small in numbers, they did exert a large amount of influence in nationalist intellectual circles and they acted as a magnet for media attention, which was always best pleased when it could illuminate the crankier side of Scottish nationalism.

The majority in the NPS, however, came from the moderate wing of Scottish nationalism. For many former SHRA members, the National Party was designed to be a catalyst in Scottish politics.[34] It was argued that all the NPS had to do was to show to the mainstream British parties, most especially the Labour Party, that Scottish home rule was popular with the electorate: 'The fact is that the most effective way to get the Labour Party or any other party to take up home rule in earnest, is to show it that votes will be lost if neglected.'[35] Once achieved, the National Party would cease to have any specific function in Scottish politics. This view contrasted with some hard-liners who argued that the NPS ought to exist as a separate party in its own right with specific social and economic policies. For many former SHRA activists, this concentration on detail was superfluous and indeed, by focusing the party's attention on specifics, it risked the alienation of potential support.[36] For others, specific policies were necessary in order to project to the electorate the practical benefits to the man and women in the street of a Scottish parliament. Without this it was argued, few would believe in the necessity of Scottish home rule.[37] Also, the moderate majority in the NPS did not believe in full blown separation from England. The preferred model was for some form of devolution which was modelled on the notion of dominion status. A Scottish parliament, it was believed, should only concern itself with domestic affairs, while the Imperial parliament would concentrate on imperial, foreign and defence policy. It was a policy which had clear lines of continuity with the pre-war home rule ideas and the suggestion that Scotland should secede from the Union was regarded with horror among most moderates.

In its initial stages, such differences of ideology and strategy were pasted over in the interests of party unity. Initial optimism that the party would do well in attracting electoral support detracted attention from the glaring and irreconcilable divisions within its ranks. Furthermore, each of the different wings believed that their view would ultimately triumph as party orthodoxy. The initial foray into electoral contests was not a resounding success. The party lost its deposit in a by election in Midlothian in February 1929, but this was put down to inexperience and a lack of resources.[38] Little progress had been made by the general election of 1931 and the party had only enough resources to contest five seats, three of which were saved deposits, but the best performance was a mere fourteen per cent in the Inverness constituency. For some, the party's greatest achievement was as a wrecking device for Labour prospects.

> As it was, the nationalist vote made it impossible for the labour man to win. I am sure that in this aspect of the matter must be giving serious thought to many of our Home Rule Labour members whose hold on their seats could ill stand the strain of a nationalist attack. It may lead them to reconsider carefully their Home Rule stand.[39]

In the Dumbartonshire by-election in March 1932, the nationalist intervention cost Tom Johnston a golden opportunity to return to parliament following Labour's route in the 1931 general election. Johnston was one of the Labour Party's most talented politicians and he was sorely missed by the opposition frontbench. As one member of the party gleefully reported: 'We saved our deposit... and kept Tom Johnston from Westminster for the present. This may cause some of our halfway Scottish nationalists to reconsider their position.'[40] This form of electoral blackmail, however, had exactly the opposite effect. Johnston was regarded as a friend to Scottish home rule and these spoiling tactics merely hardened attitudes in Labour's ranks towards the nationalists. As one Labour party member commented: 'If the national party persists in injuring and opposing all who aim at Scottish management of Scottish affairs unless they abandon all other causes than home rule, then I can safely predict the younger members of the N.P. will be mouldering in their graves and home rule still in the future.'[41] In the wake of the Great Depression and the resultant social and economic upheaval, the Labour Party argued that the aspirations of nationalists were about as far removed from the interests of working class people as it was possible to be (see chapter four).

The wrecking policy pursued by the NPS was, however, small comfort as the expected electoral breakthrough had failed to materialise. The electoral stasis induced many to reassess the National Party's strategy and objectives. The Celticists and the fundamentalist nationalists concluded that the party was failing to make progress because of the timidity of its programme. What was called for, it was argued, was a bolder and more aggressive policy. Hard-liners demanded a tougher stance on the issue of independence:[42]

> We are out for Scottish independence in the fullest sense of the term and the abrogation of English ascendancy alike in our imperial, internal and international relationship, and in every objective or subjective connection.... Any refusal to give Scotland free choice to remain or go out of the Empire, to associate freely or dis-associate itself at will from England, to share a common financial and economic policy with other nations, or to pursue a separate policy of its own, is to subject Scotland to a species of slavery, involving the assumption that the Scottish people are so stupid that they cannot be trusted for themselves for fear that they jeopardise 'wider interests'.[42]

For good measure, the fundamentalist camp began to broadcast other dubious policies which included a type of Scottish Fascism which would replace Anglo Saxon democracy.[43] Others associated with this group did not go as far, although they accepted the principle of Scottish independence. For them, the party would only attract support when the campaign for independence was aligned with specific socio-economic policies. Planning and projections of what an independent Scotland could achieve had to be promoted in order to convince the Scottish electorate that independence would raise standards of living. In short, the policy had to have relevance and that lofty notions about the virtues of freedom would fall on deaf ears, particularly when most people were concerned about poor housing, health, education and unemployment. The National Party, it was argued, would have to campaign on a platform of independence which would address these specific issues. As a consequence of this Tom Gibson and Iain Gillies set to work drafting policies related to Scottish social and economic regeneration. Among the many options propounded were plans for the revitalisation of rural Scotland through the extension of rural and forestry industries and small farming, most of which was based on Scandinavian models. The party also endeavoured to highlight aspects of British economic policy which worked to the benefit of the southern English economy, but which harmed Scottish interests. Intellectually, such efforts did much to boost the party's credibility, although the press and the public preferred to focus on the more colourful aspect of the nationalists movement and even within the ranks of the NPS, many ignored official policy.[44]

The expected political coherence which many thought would evolve failed to materialise and consensus was impossible to reach. The situation within the NPS was exacerbated in 1932 with the creation of a moderate, right-wing home rule movement, the Scottish Party. In essence, this organisation was the result of a secession from the Cathcart Unionist Association and its members believed that Scotland was being unfairly treated by indifferent government from Westminster. Furthermore, many were worried that the nationalism of the NPS was tainted with socialism, republicanism and separatism. The Scottish Party presented itself as the reasonable face of Scottish nationalism and contrasted its modest proposals for devolution with the wilder aspirations of the NPS's Celtic fringe. The description of the NPS was hardly flattering:

> Novelists, essayists and poets, rather than businessmen, were found in their ranks. Hence the insistence on such terms as 'sovereign power and independence', without much consideration as to what these ideals meant or how they were to be achieved. Other extravagances, such as 'separation from England', 'kilted sailors in Scottish ships', and 'Gaelic speaking ambassadors', got mixed up with their utopian ideals, and certainly put off much support which the party's energy would have otherwise obtained. Today the national spirit is sponsored by another 'Scottish party', based on principles moderate, reasonable and free from all hatred of England.[45]

The Scottish Party was given more favourable coverage by the press and its leaders, such as Sir Daniel Stevenson, Sir Alexander McEwan and Sir Henry Dalziel, had an aura of respectability which many moderates in the National Party craved.[46] It was the appearance of a moderate challenger to the NPS which induced a fundamental reorientation of party strategy. Moderates, such as John MacCormick, blamed the fundamentalists for tarnishing the reputation of the party. It was claimed that their brand of Celtic nationalism with its emphasis on separatism was frightening away potential support. It was argued that the National Party would have to moderate its aims or face political oblivion and with the Scottish Party in existence, there was now a potential competitor for the centre ground of Scottish nationalism. This was especially the case after the party's disastrous performance in the East Fife by election at the beginning of 1933. The nationalist candidate, Eric Linklater, was subject to a barrage of criticism from Scottish Party members who wanted to know if the NPS stood for total political separation from England. Linklater's performance was not convincing and he was evasive on a number of key issues.[47] With recent opinion polls showing support among the Scottish public for some form of home rule, the obvious explanation of the poor performance for most National Party moderates was that the extremists had damaged the credibility of the NPS. The solution, it was argued, was to moderate policy and, if possible, remove the Celticists.

The 're-statement of policy' was the most bitter episode in the short history of the NPS. Under the guidance of John MacCormick, the moderates forced through what was presented as a clarification of policy in which it was stated quite explicitly that the NPS did not seek separation from England, but rather 'self-government within the British group of nations' with Westminster retaining control of foreign, imperial and defence policy. The fundamentalists, however, refused to accept this and claimed that the party constitution was being reworked to appease the 'establishment' figures in the Scottish Party. For them it was the very timidity of the NPS which was failing to attract support and it was argued that further dilution of the party's principles and aims would only lead to emasculation. The 'strong arm' tactics of the fundamentalists who brought pressure to bear on sympathetic individuals ended up alienating potential support and at the end of the day, most members of the NPS believed that their advocacy of outright independence was unlikely to appeal to the Scottish electorate: 'Republicanism is antipathetic to the overwhelming majority of the Scottish people and cannot today be realised either by forceful or peaceful methods.'[48] For MacCormick and others, the National Party would only make headway once its objectives were brought more into line with the perceived aspirations of the Scottish people. The result was a bloodletting in which the fundamentalists were expelled. Iain and William Gillies, along with C.M. Grieve, were thrown out of the party and it set in train a process in which others, by no means all of whom belonged to the fundamentalist camp, were purged from the NPS ranks.[49]

The expulsion should not be seen as an isolated endeavour to put the National Party's ideological house in order. As early as 1932, leading moderates within the NPS were in touch with elements in the Scottish Party in order to formulate plans for greater co-operation. MacCormick in particular, was impressed by the 'establishment' credibility of his nationalist opponents and believed that if it were possible to convert more like-minded figures to the cause, then their task would be an easier one. The Scottish Party had a degree of respectability and gravity that MacCormick badly wanted and it was recognised that merger or co-operation would not be possible while the National Party harboured fundamentalists who would brook no compromise on their stand of outright independence.[50] The difference between the two organisations, it was argued, was superficial. The announcement of a by election in Kilmarnock in the Autumn of 1933 was the prelude to a merger between both parties. Initially, the NPS intended to fight the seat alone, however, the prospect of a rival Scottish Party candidate forced a hasty reassessment of the situation. It was realised that two nationalist candidates would split the potential vote and damage the credibility of the self-government cause. As the senior party, the NPS had most to lose and this was not lost on members of the Scottish Party who as yet were untried in electoral politics: 'The NPS have run into heavy weather in East Fife. They will be ridiculed and maybe open to more reason.'[51] The upshot of the intensive negotiations was that Sir Alexander MacEwen would stand as a joint candidate. MacEwen was from the Scottish Party and had the support of MacCormick who was determined to push through a merger at all costs. For many, the contest was the litmus test of the merger strategy. The score in the by election of seventeen per cent of the votes cast was the best nationalist performance to date. This limited electoral progress seemed to vindicate the policy of moderation and merger, and the launch of the Scottish National Party was carried out in April 1934 in a mood of optimism and confidence.[52]

Nationalist expectations that the SNP would emerge as the new and dynamic force in Scottish politics were soon confounded. Firstly, there was the problem that the Kilmarnock by-election had been a bit of fluke. There was no Tory candidate as part of the National Government's electoral pact and MacEwen picked up rogue votes from disgruntled Tories who would not vote for National Labour. Secondly, there were deep seated divisions of ideology and strategy. While MacCormick had blamed the lack of electoral progress of the NPS on the influence of the fundamentalists on party ideology and strategy, he did not pay too much attention the programme of the Scottish Party. If he had, he would have found it to be little more that a collection of notables who had nothing more in common than the fact that they believed something was wrong with Scotland. The Scottish Party had no coherent electoral strategy, no specific economic and social policies and, perhaps most important of all, no party organisation. Furthermore, MacCormick over-estimated the influence of its leaders. While the duke of Montrose, Andrew Dewar Gibb, Sir Daniel Stevenson and Lord Daziel might sound impressive to a party on the fringes of Scottish politics, the truth of the matter was that most of these politicians had passed their sell by date and had little influence on the mainstream of Scottish politics. Yet, MacCormick did not take this into account and when it came to deciding the senior positions within the hierarchy of the SNP, former Scottish Party officials were more than proportionally rewarded.

It did not take long for these difficulties to become apparent. By the end of 1934 a row had erupted over the activities of former Scottish Party member, Kevin MacDowall, who claimed that maintaining the integrity of the British Empire was more important than the establishment of a Scottish parliament.[53] The incident revealed much of the internal weakness of the SNP. There had been a tacit agreement that because the movement was a broad church and contained a variety of ideological persuasions, members should make their pronouncements with sensitivity.[54] MacDowall's remarks angered the left wing of the party and those who supported a more strident form of home rule. Furthermore, McDowall's sniping at the party council in the press did little to boost the image of the SNP as a united movement. Other incidents followed. The left were outraged at the duke of

Montrose's outburst against hitch hikers who he described as trespassers, and Andrew Dewar Gibb's repeated reference to those in the Labour Party as Marxists, likewise caused offence.[55] Strains also began to emerge over the direction of party policy. Given that most of rank and file of the SNP had come from the left of centre National Party, there was an expectation that this would be reflected in the policies of the SNP. Yet, in an endeavour to promote harmony and keep ideological divisions under the surface, the policies which emerged tended to be woolly and vague. Indeed, much of it was vacuous rhetoric:

> The Scottish National Party makes no appeal to class interests, to sectional or sectarian prejudices, or to worn out political creeds. It makes its stand on the urgent necessity for all men and women of goodwill in Scotland to unite in the work of national redemption.[56]

What this 'national redemption' was and how it was to be achieved received little elaboration. For many of the rank and file in the SNP, the avoidance of specific policy commitments gave the impression that the party had veered to the right.

Further problems emerged in May 1935 when the party's president, the duke of Montrose, took the unilateral decision to drop the Conservative whip in the House of Lords and join the Liberals instead.[57] This came as a bombshell as few were aware that he still held the Tory whip. Yet, it was his argument that the cause would be better served by joining the Liberals rather than acting as a solitary SNP peer which caused most dismay.[58] Montrose revealed an appalling ignorance of his own party's constitution which stated quite explicitly that members of the SNP could not be members of other political parties. Furthermore, Montrose argued that as the SNP had no specific social and economic policies, it was necessary to have some form of ideological position upon which to debate issues in the House of Lords and in this, the Liberal party was closest to his beliefs. Again, this was in frank contradiction of party policy and damaged the limited endeavours to build up a credible raft of socio-economic programmes. The incident was a very public demonstration of nationalist incoherence and it bruised party morale just before the general election of 1935. No sooner had Montrose let the cat out the bag, when other Council members, such as the popular novelist, Annie S. Swan, revealed that they were also active members of the Liberal Party.[59]

Initial hopes that the party would contest ten seats at the general election were soon confounded and the number was cut back to seven due to inadequate finances and a lack of suitable candidates. The fiasco of MacDowall's secession, Montrose's and others involvement with the Liberal Party and general disaffection among the rank and file over the party's lack of direction took its toll on morale. Although many members worked enthusiastically and hard, there was, nevertheless, an air of pessimism about the campaign. While not expecting great things, the party leadership was not prepared for the electoral set back which ensued. Nationalists had contested five of the seven seats before and in each of them their share of the vote had dropped significantly. Only in Inverness and the Western Isles, where MacCormick and MacEwan were the respective candidates, did the SNP put in, by their standards, a reasonable showing by winning sixteen and twenty eight per cent of the vote.[60] Two key issues dominated the election; the international situation and the economy, and on both fronts the SNP was weak. The nationalists had little to say other than the usual declarations in favour of collective security and peace on the question of mounting international tension. And, as we have seen, the party's economic and social programme offered little beyond platitudes when it came to addressing the question of structural economic dislocation. The party also had problems with its image. It was presented as a Tory organisation in the Labour press which focused on the duke of Montrose as the face of Scottish nationalism. In Conservative circles, it was denounced as a separatist organisation with socialist and republican leanings. Furthermore, to add insult to injury, both of the main British parties agreed that the SNP was nothing more than an eccentric collection of cranks on the fringes of Scottish political life which had little of relevance to offer to the Scottish electorate.[61]

Having failed to make an impact on Scottish electoral politics, the SNP after 1935 began to disintegrate into competing faction, all of which pursued their own particular agendas. Party discipline collapsed and it was soon apparent that the hierarchy had no control over the activities of the rank and file. Those on the left wanted to follow a more vigorous policy which would stress the party's commitment to social justice and redistributive economic policies. Roland Muirhead provided funds for the *Scots Independent* to start up again in 1935 and the journal gave space to all different types of commentators. The one thing that they all seemed to have in common, however, was criticism of the party leadership and official policy. For some, the only way to achieve a Scottish parliament was to stick at contesting elections. For others, however, the experience of the last several years had shown that this would be a long haul and some were inclined to revert back to the pressure group tactics of the SHRA. A few even suggested infiltrating and subverting the established parties from within.[62] MacCormick believed that some form of fusion with the Liberal Party might help the SNP out of its electoral morass. After all, both parties had been banished to the fringes of Scottish politics and both had a lot to lose from competing against each other. Also, MacCormick believed the Liberals to be ideologically close to the mainstream of the SNP: ' I do not think that it will do any harm to make our faith especially attractive to Liberals just now. They are nearest to us in many respects and more important, are without real leadership at the moment.'[63] There were also a number of prominent Liberals within the ranks of the SNP and the party's chairman, Sir Alexander MacEwan, never hid his Liberal leanings from the electorate. Indeed, rumours that MacEwen was toying with the idea of standing as an independent Liberal home ruler in the Ross and Cromarty by election in 1936 brought a tirade of denunciation from left wingers and those committed to the principle of fighting elections.[64] Such was the furore that MacEwen felt compelled to offer his resignation.[65]

The failure of Scottish nationalism to emerge as a coherent political force led many former members of the Scottish Party to lose interest and this was reflected in their dwindling attendance at council meetings. The expectation that establishment figures would lend credibility to the SNP and pay electoral dividends was cruelly misplaced. Although a few brave souls soldiered on, most notably the new party chairman, Andrew Dewar Gibb, the infusion of the Scottish Party into the National Party was now reckoned to be a mistake:

The tampering of the wording of the object and policy which began in 1932 and culminated with the fusion of the National Party of Scotland and the Scottish Party, must be held as responsible for the weakening of the enthusiasm of its members... (the) results of this were the resignations from the party of a number of hard working and enthusiastic Scottish Nationalists, the expulsion of others and the incoming into the SNP of some very moderate Nationalists. But more damaging to the Party was its act in putting at its head a member of the Scottish nobility (the duke of Montrose), that relic of the past, an action distasteful to the democracy of Scotland.[66]

The left was no longer content to remain silent and began an onslaught against the right. Party discipline had collapsed, there was no ideological coherence and there was no clear political strategy. For many stalwarts in the SNP, it appeared as if the infusion of the Scottish Party into their ranks was responsible for diluting the nationalist movement out of existence.

It was in this atmosphere of chaos and confusion that the left of the party sought to reassert a more radical and disciplined programme. It was thought that the appeal to the middle-classes was fruitless and that attention ought to be focused on the working-class:

Those who engineered the fusion of the NPS and the SP surely could not have recognised that if the party was to grow, it must look to do so from Labour voters, since Unionists and Liberals (what is left of them) are afraid of home rule as they see quite clearly that if Scotland gets self-government she will have a radical and Labour government, and they hate the idea of Socialism in power.[67]

The left set to work in drafting economic and social policies which were designed to appeal to the working-class, and, by virtue of numbers and enthusiasm, was able to ensure their endorsement by the National Council. The left, although by no means all of them, sought to use such policies as part of a wider programme to reassert the party's political distinctiveness. Also, it was believed that the SNP would have to tighten up its discipline, reassert the principle that members could not belong to other political parties or organisations and, most importantly, continue to contest elections in order to obtain a mandate for self-government. This was pushed through in the face of opposition from the right and Andrew Dewar Gibb lamented the reappearance, as he described it, of republican and socialist tendencies within the party. The decision that the SNP would support the anti-Fascist League was not endorsed by Gibb who viewed the episode as another endeavour by a subversive group of socialists to lurch the party to the left. To add insult to injury, many of the sacred totems of the right were increasingly denounced in the radical's journal, the *Scots Independent.* Left wingers such as Archie Lamont denounced Dewar Gibb's anti-Irish prejudices and along with Oliver Brown, campaigned against him as the official nationalist candidate in the Universities by-election of 1938. The British Empire came under increasing fire and support was given to Irish republicans in radical circles. The fundamentalists which had been expelled in from the NPS in 1932 began to creep back into the movement due to the party's loose discipline and ambiguous constitution. The endorsement of an anti-conscription policy at the annual conference in 1937, confirmed to many the ascendancy of the radical wing in the SNP.[68]

As if the ideological divisions were not bad enough, the party was equally fragmented over strategy. The failure to make an electoral impact had led many to denounce the policy of contesting elections and the decision was taken that this avenue would only be pursued selectively.[69] The principal reason why the radicals were able to have so many of their policies officially adopted by the party was that, to all intents and purposes, those who believed that the SNP should act as a pressure group paid little attention to those who tried to beef up the SNP's credibility as an independent political organisation. J.M. MacCormick had come to the conclusion that the best way forward for Scottish self-government was to adopt a cross party approach and establish a National Convention which would act as a catalyst in making the mainstream parties take the issue seriously. By the late thirties, MacCormick was more interested in building bridges to others in different political organisations than scrutinising what was going on in his own party. In this endeavour, he was given hope by the fact that

Labour seemed to be softening its attitude to Scottish nationalism and was once again expressing interest in setting up a parliament in Edinburgh (see Chapter Four). The collapse of the SNP as a credible political party meant that it was clearly unable to influence the outcome of any by elections. This led many in the Labour Party to toy again with the idea of Scottish home rule. As far as MacCormick was concerned, this was a better window of opportunity than any changes to SNP policy and in January 1939, after two years of negotiations, the existence of the National Convention was announced.[70] MacCormick was unconcerned by the leftward drift of SNP policy as it was decided that the party would not contest more than five seats at a general election, and as such, it was of little practical consequence.[71] The radicals were given a free hand in policy formulation because the SNP was unable to electorally threaten either the Liberal or Labour parties. It was this, more than SNP policy, which was the essential part of MacCormick's strategy of keeping his Convention partners sweet. Also, as former members of the Scottish Party gradually drifted away from the NPS, with the exception of Andrew Dewar Gibb and Robert Hurd, there was no effective right wing opposition to the radicals who were able to monopolise party policy by the late thirties.

By the eve of the Second World War, the SNP was collapsing under the strain of its own internal contradictions. The party contained disparate factions, each of which pursued its own agenda and so long as there was no interference from others, this state of affairs was allowed to continue. In any case, the collapse of any kind of effective party discipline meant that there was little that could be done by the National Executive to try and enforce some form of cohesion. Things came to a crunch with the outbreak of the Second World War in September 1939. The party had adopted an anti-conscription programme as official policy and it was expected by many that this should be followed to the letter.[72] This, however, went against the legalist wing of the party which soon took cold feet and argued that in view of the national emergency, such a policy would be disastrous and harm nationalist credibility.[73] MacCormick had scheduled the first meeting of the National Convention for September 1939 and was worried that die hard nationalist attitudes would wreck his attempts to reach some kind of rapprochement with the Labour and Liberal parties.

Andrew Dewar Gibb made impassioned pleas for further negotiations between the British and German governments, believing that Communism and the Soviet Union were a greater threat to world civilisation than Fascism.[74] Most members, it has to be said, were confused, as no clear leadership or strategy emerged. It would be harder to find a more complete picture of indecision and incoherence in any other political organisation at this time. It would take several years of war and internal party conflict before the SNP was to attain the necessary degree of internal discipline and political coherence necessary for an effective political organisation.

NOTES

[1] *H.C. Debs.*, col. 2076, 16 April 1920.

[2] STUC Annual Report 1918.

[3] See R.J. Finlay, *Independent and Free: Scottish Politics and the Origins of the Scottish National Party, 1918-45*, (Edinburgh, 1994), pp. 8-10.

[4] Michael Keating and David Bleiman, *Labour and Scottish Nationalism*, (London, 199), pp. 79-101.

[5] *Self-Determination for Scotland*, (Glasgow, 1919).

[6] See I.G.C. Hutchison, *A Political History of Modern Scotland, 1832-1924: Parties, Elections and Issues*, (Edinburgh, 1986), pp. 309-33.

[7] Finlay, *Independent and Free*, pp. 16-18.

[8] *Scottish Home Rule*, April 1924, pp. 74-75.

[9] *ibid.*

[10] *Scottish Home Rule*, April 1924, p.74.

[11] Hutchison, *Political History*, pp. 207-309.

[12] Finlay, *Independent and Free*, pp. 6-7.

[13] NLS, Acc. 6058, Box 1., R.E. Muirhead to Tom Gibson, 17 April 1924.

[14] *Scottish Home Rule*, April 1924.

[15] D. Marquand, *Ramsay MacDonald*, (London, 1977), p. 23.

[16] *Scotsman*, 10 May 1924.

[17] *Glasgow Herald*, 10 May 1924.

[18] *Scottish Home Rule*, June 1924, p. 105.

[19] NLS, Acc. 3721, Box 81, 'Minutes of the Scottish National Convention'.

[20] *ibid.*

[21] *Scottish Home Rule*, Aug. 1926, p. 19.

[22] *ibid.*, Dec. 1925, p. 54.

[23] *Ibid.*

[24] *Scotsman*, 8 May 1927.

[25] *Scottish Home Rule*, April 1927, p. 83.

[26] NLS, Acc. 6058, A.L. Henry, Secretary of the National Party Group, to Tom Gibson, 13 May 1927.

[27] NLS, Acc. 3721, Box 81, 'Records of the Scottish National Convention', May 1927, p. 23.

[28] *Scottish Home Rule*, July 1924, p. 7.

[29] NLS, Acc. 3721, Box 81, 'Records of the Scottish National Convention', Nov. 1927.

[30] *Scots Independent*, April 1928, pp. 81-83.

[31] See Finlay, *Independent and Free.*

[32] See R.J. Finlay, 'For or Against?: Scottish Nationalists and the British Empire, 1918-1939', *Scottish Historical Review*, 191/2 (1992), pp. 184-206.

[33] See Finlay, *Independent and Free*, pp. 29-71.

[34] R.J. Finlay, 'Pressure Group or Political Party?: The Nationalist Impact on Scottish Politics, 1928-45', *20th Century British History*, 3 (1993), pp. 274-98.

[35] *Scottish Home Rule*, August 1926, p. 17.

[36] Finlay, *Independent and Free*, pp. 71-2.

[37] *ibid.*, pp. 76-9.

[38] *Scots Independent*, March 1929, p. 58.

[39] NLS, Acc. 3721, Box 5, A.W, Donaldson to R.E. Muirhead, 8 Dec. 1930.

[40] *ibid.*, R.E. Muirhead to J.M. MacDiarmid, 29 March 1932.

[41] *Ibid.*, J.M. MacDiarmid to R.E. Muirhead, 6 April 1932.

[42] C.M. Grieve (Hugh MacDairmid), *Scots Independent*, June 1932, p. 116.

[43] See Finlay, *Independent and Free*, pp. 78-88.

[44] *Ibid.*

[45] The Duke of Montrose, *Self-Government for Scotland*, (Glasgow, 1933), pp. 4-5.

[46] See the *Daily Record*, Aug. 1932.

[47] For press cuttings of the campaign see NLS, Acc. 7295, file 2.

[48] NLS, Gunn Mss., Box 15, Neil M. Gunn to T.H. Gibson, 3 April 1933.

[49] See Finlay, *Independent and Free*, pp. 117-19.

[50] *ibid.*

[51] NLS, Gibb Mss., Dep. 207, Box 2, G.M. Thomson to A.D. Gibb, 20 Jan. 1933.

[52] See Finlay, *Independent and Free*, pp. 126-162.

[53] *Weekly Herald,* 10 Dec. 1934.

[54] NLS, Acc. 3721, Box, 11, R.E. Muirhead to A.D. Gibb, 1 Feb. 1935.

[55] Finlay, *Independent and Free*, pp. 165-83.

[56] *Scots Independent,* July 1934, p. 135.

[57] *Glasgow Herald*, 4 May 1935.

[58] NLS, Dep. 209, Box 15, Montrose to N.L. Gunn, 15 July 1935.

[59] Minute Book of the National Council of the SNP, June 1935.

[60] Finlay, *Independent and Free*, pp. 183-4.

[61] Finlay, 'Pressure Group or Political Party'.

[62] See Finlay, *Independent and Free*, pp. 184-99.

[63] NLS, Acc. 6508, Box 1, J.M. MacCormick to Tom Gibson, 7 Feb. 1935.

[64] *Scots Independent*, Jan. 1936.

[65] Minute Book of the National Council of the SNP, 7 Feb. 1936.

[66] *Scots Independent*, Feb. 1936, p. 2.

[67] *ibid.*

[68] Finlay, *Independent and Free*, pp. 184-99.

[69] NLS, Acc. 6580, Box 1, A.D. Gibb to Elma Gibson, 12 May 1936.

[70] Minute Book of the National Council of the SNP, Jan. 1939.

[71] *ibid.*

[72] NLS, Young Mss. Box 44, 'Report of the Annual Conference of the SNP, 1939'.

[73] *ibid.*

[74] *Scots Independent*, Oct. 1939, p.1.

CHAPTER FOUR

The Unionist Response: Dependency and the Rise of Centralism, 1918-1939

The First World War fundamentally changed the political, social, economic and cultural landscape of Scotland. In terms of politics, the early twenties witnessed the gradual disintegration of the once mighty Liberal Party which found itself squeezed out between the twin pressures of a vibrant Labour Party and a reconstituted Unionist Party.[1] The Liberals were hampered by internal division and their endeavours to chart a centre course through the hazards of a political terrain marked with class polarisation proved fruitless. The Labour Party found that it was the prime beneficiary of a sharpened sense of working-class political consciousness which had been engendered by an enlarged and confident trade union movement, conflict over rents, wages, living and working conditions and the effect of the Fourth Reform Act which finally extended the vote to all adult males and women over thirty.[2] After the general election of 1922, Labour emerged as the largest single party in Scotland. The Unionists, who had been pessimistic as to their prospects before the First World War, found that the climate of Scottish politics after 1918 was altogether more hospitable. Industrial militancy and Bolshevik Revolution in Europe had sharpened middle-class fears about the threat of socialism and it was the Unionist Party, especially after Liberal support for a minority Labour government in 1924, which was the prime beneficiary of this. Indeed, it was the middle-class which displayed the greater degree of class solidarity and political mobilisation during the tumult of war and it was the Unionist Party which was best placed to harness this.[3] The 'die hard' image of the Edwardian era was toned down as the party made its appeal to the enlarged farming community, women and the young. With the Liberals pushed out of the way, Scottish politics after 1924 settled down to a brief period of two party politics based predominantly on class interests.

The Scottish economy, which was hailed as the 'workshop of the Empire' in the pre-war era was in deep trouble. The failings of structural imbalance were cruelly exposed after 1918 in a world where the economic priorities of the global market shifted away from Scotland's traditional heavy industries.[4] There was a glut of ships, and in any case, the Americans could now build them cheaper. Without ships, there was no need for steel or marine engineering. Markets for coal in Easter Europe had been lost during the war, as had the Indian jute market. Reparations and a dislocated world economy meant that there was less demand for the capital investment goods, such as heavy engineering, ships and locomotives, which had been produced in great abundance by the Scottish economy before 1914. The limited diversification into new industries which had taken place in the Scottish economy before the war was wiped out as industrialists went hell for leather into armament production in order to capitalise on the easy profits which could be made on wartime munitions. Obviously such profound economic dislocation meant social dislocation. In addition to the long term problems of poor health, housing and poverty which had plagued pre-war Scottish society, some new ones were added after 1918. Long term mass unemployment scarred the Scottish social landscape throughout the inter-war period and decimated whole communities. Although historians have a fondness for recounting average unemployment figures, the truth of the matter is that there was no average. Statistically, to be unemployed usually meant living in a community with about thirty to forty per cent unemployment, rather than the notional average of thirteen per cent. In the twenties and thirties, comparative figures with England on socio-economic performance told a doleful story of persistent Scottish under-achievement. All of which led many contemporaries to talk about the 'end of Scotland' as the nation appeared to be caught fast in a process of terminal decline.[5]

Although the inter-war period witnessed the flowering of the Scottish renaissance, most Scots at the time thought that a distinctive Scottish culture was doomed to extinction.[6] According to one critic, the Scots were a dying race. Fears of uncontrolled Irish immigration, tales of razor gangs in Glasgow, the southward drift of Scottish industry, emigration and falling population, the persistence of slum housing and a massive outpouring of tracts and books on the condition of Scotland told a rather different tale. Far from cultural regeneration in the twenties and thirties, most Scots believed their society was in a state of terminal national disintegration.[7] All these factors contributed to a mood of cultural pessimism in Scottish intellectual and political circles and it is against this backdrop that debates about Scotland's place in the Union were carried out.

Home Rule and Political Realignment

The First World War had killed off Sir Henry Cowan's 1913 Scottish home rule bill. While many expected that the situation in 1918 could take off from where it had been suspended in 1914, the reality was that circumstances had changed. Firstly, the Unionists were in a stronger position in 1918 and had put in the best performance of all the parties in the general election in Scotland of that year. Their attitude towards Scottish home rule was one of hostility, and given the fact that many Liberals, both independent and coalition, were dependent on Unionist support to keep their parliamentary seats safe from the Labour onslaught, it comes as no surprise to find that the issue had little momentum in Unionist and Liberal circles. This view was perhaps best summed up by Robert Munro, Coalition Liberal Scottish Secretary and former Young Scot, who declined to take part in any campaign for a Scottish parliament on the grounds that it would be inappropriate for a member of the government to do so.[8] This apathy and disinterest was illustrated at a Speakers Conference in Westminster on Devolution where one Unionist MP declared that Scotland was no longer a nation, having 'passed through the state of nationhood. Her nationhood has been absorbed in a wider area.'[9] Nationalism had been given a bad press during the war and Walter Elliot, a rising star of the Unionist Party, claimed that Scottish home rule would revive the 'spirit of chauvinist nationalism which has swept Europe like a pestilence for these last four years.'[10] In any case, few Scottish MPs turned up to support the second reading of Cowan's pre-war bill and it was counted out much to the chagrin of the SHRA.[11] Most Unionists reiterated their pre-war arguments against home rule and claimed that it would be inefficient, expensive, and not worth the candle. Also, it was claimed that the demand for a parliament did not come from the people but was in fact whipped up by a minority of enthusiasts who claimed to represent the will of the Scottish people, but who were in fact only promoting their own interests. However, given that the Unionists dominated the

Coalition government, there was little likelihood of it being given much parliamentary attention.

The advent of Labour as the biggest parliamentary party in Scotland after the general election in 1922 meant that the issue could not be ignored in Unionists circles as home rule appeared to be endorsed with enthusiasm and commitment by many leading Labour politicians. Before boarding for the train to Westminster in 1922, John Wheatley told an audience that 'there was no subject in Scotland that arouses as much enthusiasm as that of home rule.'[12] Labour's commitment to the policy bound up home rule, in the mind of Unionists, as part of the programme of the left. The SHRA was portrayed as a front for socialism and this was especially the case as the trade unions and the Labour Party tightened their control over the Association's activities. The creation of a Scottish parliament was presented as method of securing socialism in Scotland through the backdoor. One of the few Conservatives who expressed an interest in the activities of the SHRA, Sir Henry Keith, a former Lord Provost of Hamilton, soon left when it became apparent that the Association was dominated by the labour movement.[13] Another part of the Unionist armoury against Scottish home rule was the experience of Ireland. In that country the home rule experiment had gone disastrously wrong with demands for constitutional reform ending up in military conflict and civil war. According to one Unionist, Ireland should be a salutory lesson for all Scottish home rulers: 'If you want to transfer all the difficulties of Ireland to Scotland, then the best way to do it would be to adopt this measure (of home rule).'[14] This was a sensitive issue even among members of the SHRA who went out of their way to deny that there was any comparability between the Scottish and Irish experience.[15] The Unionist Party exploited this and held up 'that unhappy island' as a warning against constitutional do-gooders.

The failure of George Buchanan's Bill in 1924 was the occasion of further Unionist denouncement of Scottish home rule aspirations. The press dismissed the bill as an absurd project and the scenes of parliamentary disruption which followed in its wake further reinforced notions that Scottish home rule was the narrow preserve of unthinking cranks.[16] While the failure of this bill may have allayed Conservative fears, it did, however, help to initiate a critical reassessment of Scottish home rule in Labour intellectual circles. It was no secret that the party leadership was lukewarm to say the least, and that in terms of priorities, it had a fairly low ranking. The prime minister, Ramsay MacDonald, gave some sense of its importance to the Labour Party leadership in a letter to Roland Muirhead:

> I am afraid at the present moment it is impossible for me with all the burdens of straightening out matters, to go into all the details about Scottish home rule. I am covered up under suggestions from my friends about everything that ranges from the most important matters to the most insignificant. You will all have to keep me out for a while until I make general arrangements, and then I will come in and tackle details. In any event, the man who would have to handle the matter, first of all at any rate, would be the head to the responsible department.[17]

The premier was a busy man and Scottish home rule demands would have to take their place in the queue behind other more pressing priorities. Furthermore, some of the clauses in Buchanan's bill were ambiguous and the possibility existed that MPs from Scotland would have to be reduced or withdrawn from Westminster as part of a wider constitutional settlement. Given that Scotland was regarded as a Labour stronghold, this did not make sense as any reduction in Scottish MPs would more than likely mean a reduction in Labour MPs. This was not acceptable to a party forming a minority government. It needed all the MPs it could get. Indeed, as one of the keenest proponents of the bill, David Kirkwood, claimed, Scotland was more radical than England and Scottish MPs were needed to give Westminster a more progressive composition.[18]

Labour endorsed Scottish home rule in the early twenties as part of a wider baggage of radical reform. It was a tenet of belief that had been inherited from the Liberal Party and few gave it any serious thought. Furthermore, as was demonstrated in chapter two, home rule was primarily promoted as a means to wider social reform in Scotland in the Edwardian period, and, therefore, it should come as no surprise to find that it enjoyed widespread support in the labour movement. While there was no doubting Labour's emotional commitment to

Scottish home rule, the same could not be said of its intellectual commitment. Most of Labour's espousal of Scottish self-government was a rehash of old Liberal policies. Indeed, this was not unique to home rule and was a feature of most Labour policy, and it is perhaps only because the issue came to a crunch in 1924 that many were forced to think through the ramifications and implications of home rule. In the long-term, a number of factors worked against the issue becoming a key aspect of Labour's Scottish programme. Reform of party organisation and structure in 1926 stamped more central discipline on the movement and worked against national and geographical sectarianism.[19] Initial hostility to Westminster mellowed among the proponents of Scottish home rule within the parliamentary Labour Party, most particularly the Clydesiders. They became more comfortable with the strange rituals of life in Westminster as time wore on. On arrival at Westminster they had experienced a culture shock and retreated into a defensive Scottish mentality as one way of coping with this daunting experience. By the late twenties, however, they had emerged as deft hands at parliamentary procedure and protocol.[20]

The attitude of the Scottish Trade Union Congress was also instrumental in the reassessment of Labour's commitment to Scottish home rule. The STUC had been in favour of a Scottish parliament as a way of defending the rights and autonomy of smaller Scottish unions against the predatory and centralising tendencies of larger British unions. However, following the set back of the General Strike in 1926 and a worsening economic climate, many Scottish trade unionist began to see the opportunities for protection in larger British unions as a better guarantee of safety. Small Scottish unions would be vulnerable and easily picked off by employers and compared to the grim reality of job losses and worsening conditions and pay, the sacrifice of Scottish autonomy seemed a small price to pay.[21] The economic realities of the late twenties cost the Scottish home rule movement one of its most persistent and reliable allies.

The principle intellectual determinant in reorienting Labour attitudes towards Scottish home rule, however, came from John Wheatley. He was among the few socialists, Oswald Mosely was another, to address the practical problems facing a socialist government in a world capitalist system.[22] Wheatley concluded that any socialist government would face hostility from capitalist nations which would do their utmost to bring about the downfall of the regime. It was necessary, he argued, that socialist governments adopt policies which would enable them to withstand a siege of international capitalism. In many ways, this was a 'socialism in one country' philosophy and in terms of economic and social policy, the state would have to direct and coordinate planning. Wheatley wanted to utilise the full resources of the British nation and Empire to regenerate British economy and society and turn it into a self-sustaining and self-reliant socialist state. Obviously, this had major implications for a policy of Scottish home rule. Given that one of the primary reasons for the creation of a parliament in Edinburgh had been to institute social and economic reform, Wheatley's ideas rendered this vital aspect of Scottish home rule redundant. If social and economic improvement was to come from central planning directed from Westminster, a Scottish parliament would have little to do. Furthermore, as the twenties wore on and Scotland's social and economic problems appeared to becoming more and more intractable, it was assumed that there was not the indigenous capacity to effectively deal with the scale of the problem. Scottish economic and social dislocation was of such a magnitude that it could only be solved by calling on the full resources of the British state.

Scottish social problems were more or less the exclusive property of the working-class, which suffered most as a result of the economic dislocation. Infant mortality rates did not decline to the same extent as those for England and Wales. Medical opinion acknowledged that the average Scot was in a poorer physical condition and overcrowding was six times greater than England.[23] Given that Labour was primarily a working-class interest party, social and economic problem solving increasingly occupied more of the party's thinking. This trend was reinforced further due to the ravages of the Great Depression in 1929.[24] Protecting the living standards of their working-class constituents was the Labour Party's immediate priority and consequently, the primacy of economics over politics dominated Labour thinking. According to James Maxton: 'The general social problem always takes premier place in my mind, before the nationalist or political changes, and I do not think that I am likely to change in that respect'.[25] Until the fundamental social and economic problems facing Scottish society had been addressed, there was no point in having a Scottish parliament. In the words of Thomas Johnston: 'What purport would there be in our getting a Scottish Parliament in Edinburgh if it has to administer an emigration system, a glorified poor law and a desert'.[26] In 1929, Ramsay MacDonald argued that the United Kingdom could not be broken up into separate economic units because it would work to the extreme disadvantage of the Scots who needed England's economic clout.[27] The STUC, while still nominally committed to the idea of home rule warned its members in 1931 that Scotland as an independent economic unit could not survive on its own and that salvation would only come from using the British state.[28] The former home ruler, David Kirkwood, chimed in with the economic unfeasibility chorus in 1933 and claimed that: 'Scotland for the Scots was so much rubbish... The idea of having nationalism and shutting out Scotland from the rest of Britain and the world was so much nonsense.'[29] The scale of the Scottish problems had grown to such an extent that only the powers of Westminster could solve it. This, however, was unacceptable to many who, as we have seen in chapter three, went off to form the National Party of Scotland in 1928.

The appearance of a hostile nationalist party did little to soften Labour attitudes to Scottish home rule.[30] It had the oppsite effect and merely encouraged anti-devolutionists in the party to condemn the whole project as absurd. The NPS was dismissed as a middle-class organisation which was designed to distract the working-class from 'the only two realities in politics, left wing socialism and right wing Toryism'.[31] Nationalism was denounced for its bourgeois origins and its lack of relevance to working-class interests. Cynics, such as Emmanuel Shinwell, claimed that demands for home rule were fuelled by romantic notions: 'These home rulers must be quite clear, and not have their policy wrapped in mysticism ... a parliament in Edinburgh might be quite useful, but he was not going to see Scotland, England and Wales divorced.'[32] Arthur Woodburn described home rule as 'mostly romance and colourful pageantry' while Patrick Dollan, Lord Provost of Glasgow and formidable party organiser, dismissed the NPS as 'a mutual admiration society for struggling poets and novelists and of no use to the working-class'.[33]

As was mentioned earlier, the cold winds which blew in with the onset of the Great Depression in 1929 had a traumatic effect on Scottish society. The Scottish economy had not being doing well in the twenties, yet few anticipated the social dislocation which followed in its wake. For the Labour Party it merely confirmed them in the belief of the primacy of economics over politics. Initially, the Conservatives had little to fear from the National Party of Scotland. It was regarded as socialist and republican and in any case, most of the nationalist ire appeared to be directed at the Labour Party. Nationalists had no interest in wooing Conservatives, who likewise, returned the complement. As we have seen, much of the impetus behind the creation of an independent nationalist party was the belief that if Labour could be shown that votes would be lost if home rule was not taken seriously, the party would soon recant and take up the issue in earnest. The NPS was a left of centre party and deliberately targeted Labour supporters. If this was not bad enough, the NPS took advantage of the political crisis of 1931 in which, during the election of that year, the Labour Party was more or less wiped out, to act as a spoiler for Labour prospects (see chapter three). Nationalist interventions were a most unwelcome phenomenon for the Labour Party which was desperately trying to build up its organisational and parliamentary base following the crushing defeat of 1931. Compared to the problems faced by Labour after 1931, home rule die-hards were a minor irritation. Far from bringing Labour round to taking Scottish home rule seriously, the spoining tactics of the NPS alienated many former sympathisers, such as Johnston and James Barr. The crisis of 1931 had cost Labour some of its best parliamentarians and minor aspects of policy were insignificant compared to the task of organisational rebuilding which had to be undertaken. Labour politicians in the early thirties also came to the conclusion that nationalism was being supported by the middle-class and therefore remote from any potential Labour supporters. According to George Buchanan: 'It is in the main middle-class .... far greater than home rule for Scotland or for England or Ireland are the great fundamental economic problems, the problems of a community which is producing untold wealth and untold poverty.'[34] Nationalists were accused of anti-Irish sentiment to boot and David Kirkwood objected to 'the whole time of this house (of Commons) being taken up, because to me Home Rule for Scotland is a mere bagatelle compared with the situation which the country is faced.'[35] The primacy of British economic planning and the electoral strategy of the nationalist parties ensured that home rule would not receive a sympathetic hearing in Labour circles for most of the decade.

Unionism and Dependency

Just as attitudes in the Labour Party were hardening towards Scottish home rule, the Unionist Party found itself having to address increasing nationalist criticism. Whereas nationalism was identified as being a force of the left in the twenties, by the early thirties, however, it was increasingly associated with the right. The depression bit hard into many of Scotland's traditional middle-classes and, as was frequently pointed out by the press, the Scots were baring a greater brunt of the hardship than their southern neighbours. Furthermore, such criticisms could not be dismissed as the outpourings of nationalist cranks. According to Sir John Samuel:

The changes which have taken place in the spheres of shipping, shipbuilding, railways, banks, steel, manufacturing, bleaching and calico printing, the drapery and soft goods trade, chemical manufacture and even philanthropy, with the extinction of many Glasgow firms and the falling of others under English control. There has been an insidious campaign of supression of Scottish affairs for too long.[36]

The National Government in Scotland faced a particular dilemma. The policies it pursued were designed to ensure its electoral hegemony in the south of England. Low interest rates and cheap credit did much to promote the economy of the south by stimulating a building boom and providing customers for the consumer durable industries. This had little impact on the north: 'Many of the concerns which attract new capital and pay big dividends are distributive, non industrial and, so far as export trade is concerned, non productive ... these lucrative enterprises tend to concentrate more and more in the south east of England'.[37] Indeed, given this skewing of the economy, many industries and companies left Scotland to move to the more attractive and prosperous markets of the south. Traditional Unionist allies such as the Chambers of Commerce of both Glasgow and Edinburgh complained bitterly at this bias in government economic policy and demanded action to redress the balance: 'A Scotland functioning as a real controlling centre of industry, trade, agriculture, shipping and finance is a bigger asset to the British Empire and a more profitable customer to England, France and Germany and so forth, than a Scotland written all over with the words 'branch economy'.[138] Newspapers chimed in with the chorus of how the nation was unfairly treated: 'Scotland is being bled white by a process of rationalisation, more or less in the interests of England'.[39] While few commentators advocated a move towards political nationalism, all of them recognised the legitimacy of Scottish grievances:

> There is, however, a widespread discontent with economic conditions in Scotland. We see business leaving our country. London is more and more becoming the centre of finance, law, literature and the arts. More and more ambitious Scotsmen are being attracted by the glittering prizes that London can offer. So far as manual workers are concerned, our old industries stagnate and few new ones are rising up; there is unemployment and discouragement. In contrast, the new industrial areas which have London as their centre have never been so prosperous.[40]

These was not the voice of the disaffected left, nor the nationalist fringe, but traditional Unionist supporters. The Unionist Party could not ignore them.

The government response to the crisis of the early thirties was threefold. Firstly, the ideological underpinning of Unionism was transformed. The notion of the Union as an equal partnership between Scotland and England was jettisoned and replaced by one in which Scotland was dependent on the wealthier and more powerful neighbour. Secondly, Scottish national sentiment was to be acknowledged and gratified within the confines of the Union. More would be done to make the Scots feel that their national identity was safe and important. Thirdly, to counteract political nationalism, administrative devolution was used to make the Scots feel closer to the government and, it was hoped, make it more efficient. This was to be achieved without surrendering any political power from Westminster.

In their analysis of the source of Scottish national grievances and the emergence of nationalist discontent, Unionist politicians had no doubt that the economic crisis was at the heart of the matter. Sir Robert Horne claimed that Scottish nationalism:

> has received its chief importance in those communities in Scotland which are most distressed, and I believe that the present movement really had its origin in the state of great depression into which Scottish communities have fallen.... There is a sense of defeat amongst a considerable portion of the population, to which Scottish people are not accustomed. There is a feeling of a loss of pride, which may be unjustified, but nevertheless it is there and ought to be dealt with.[41]

This sentiment was echoed by the Scottish Secretary of State, Sir Godfrey Collins, who agreed that 'the depression has caused many minds to seek a solution to their problems by the setting up of a parliament in Edinburgh'.[42] Others were also of the opinion that Scotland was neglected:

> I venture to think that Scotland is not receiving sufficient consideration. Scotland has her own special problems which demand special treatment and special legislation... I cannot rid my mind of the feeling that Scotland does not receive her due share of parliamentary time.[43]

Unionists were forced to acknowledge the legitimacy of nationalist concerns and the fact that compared to other parts of the United Kingdom, the depression was taking a greater toll. The figures produced and widely circulated made grim reading. In 1932 some 400,000 or 26.2 per cent of the insured work force was idle and new industries were not coming north to offset job losses in the traditional heavy industries. In 1932, twenty new factories opened and thirty six closed, in 1933, fourteen opened and twenty nine closed; in 1934-5, thirty eight opened and fifty eight closed. The picture in the industrial west was even bleaker and Scottish industrial production in 1931 was smaller than 1913.[44] The fear of many Unionist politicians was that such economic pressures would crystallise into a nationalist movement of considerable strength. After all, this was the norm in continental Europe and opinion polls conducted by the press revealed that support for a Scottish parliament was increasing.

Whereas nationalism in the past was dismissed as the preserve of cranks and romantics, Unionist politicians were especially concerned at the type of people who were now being attracted to the nationalist movement. According to John Buchan, Scottish nationalism was in danger of spreading beyond its traditional boundaries:

It is also found among young people who are heard headed, practical and ambitious, who are shaping out for themselves careers in medicine and law and in business. Very few of that class would agree for a moment to any of the schemes of home rule at present put forward, but they all feel this dissatisfaction. They all believe that something is wrong with Scotland and that it is the business of Scotsmen to put it right.... This feeling has spread also to certain classes who have left their youth behind. The discontent of some of the small burghs with the Local Government Act of 1929 has caused many people, to whom home rule would have been an anathema, to question in measured terms the wisdom of the whole present system. The feeling has not gone far in the working class. They have grimmer things to think about. On the whole it has not affected the business community to any large extent. But it has infected a very important class who do a good deal of the thinking of the nation. I would have this House remember that it is not any scheme put forward that matters. Those schemes may be crude and foolish enough in all conscience. It is the instinct behind it that matters and unless we face that instinct honestly and fairly, we may drive it underground and presently it will appear in some irrational and dangerous form.[45]

As can be seen from the above quotation, Buchan was also aware that it was traditional Unionist voters who were in danger of infection from the nationalist movement. The appearance of the Scottish party in 1932 was a shock to Unionist complacency. This was a secession from the Cathchart Unionist Association, led by Kevin MacDowall, because it was believed that Scotland was suffering neglect from Westminster. The *Daily Record* came close to giving an endorsement of nationalist aspiration and its editor R.D. Anderson, claimed that much right was on the nationalist side.[46] Traditional Unionist allies such as the *Glasgow Herald* and the *Scotsman* were increasingly hostile to government policy and there was a perceptible rise of nationalism in their criticism:

> This transference of the control of Scottish industry is no new thing; but it has received an additional impetus from the present popularity of what is known as rationalisation. It is a movement which is fraught with the most serious consequences to Scotland, and has already caused great loss of work to Scottish people, beside limiting enormously the possibility of future expansion when trade improves ... Scottish conditions, both industrial and administrative, present their own problems. Continuance of the fundamentally false policy of centralising everything on London, will, sooner or later, finish Scotland as a nation and reduce her to a mere province of England.[47]

Followers of the Scottish Party were drawn from the mainstream of Scottish politics and figures such as Andrew Dewar Gibb and George Malcolm Thomson were as close to traditional Scottish Toryism as was possible to be. The extent of Unionist alarm at this perceived rise in Scottish nationalism was the so-called 'ragman's roll' which was a declaration against Scottish home rule by every titled and prominent Scot that the Unionist establishment could lay its hands on. The fact that this was accomplished in a short space of time and given extensive publicity, reveals the extent of Unionist concerns.[48] Yet, the problem facing the Unionists was that while all were in agreement that the depression was the source of nationalist discontent and that this discontent was quite legitimate and honourable, it was recognised that there was little that could be done to solve the problem of economic dislocation. The economic orthodoxy of the day was for as little government intervention in the economy as possible and where it was deemed necessary, it was designated to the traditional Conservative heartland in the south. Scottish industrialists pursued a wait and see policy in the belief, or hope, that things would pick up once again. Most were reluctant to diversify into new industrial sectors.[49] Unionist strategy was based on the premise that there was little that could be done on the economic front.

Nationalist claims that a parliament in Edinburgh would help the Scottish economy were dismissed and a great deal of Unionist pronouncements on the issue were simply a refutation of SNP claims. It was argued by the former Chancellor of the Exchequer, Sir Robert Horne, that a Scottish parliament would not make any difference to the Scottish economic crisis.[50] The problem was diagnosed in terms of a world depression in which governments were helpless. Horne also poured cold water on the claim that Scotland's unemployment crisis was greater than other parts of the United Kingdom by arguing that the north of England and Wales had been more severely hit. Furthermore, it was claimed that the Union allowed unemployment to be dealt with fairly and compassionately by ensuring the fair distribution of money from the richer parts of the kingdoms to help out the poorer.[51] Industrialists, likewise, chimed in with this chorus and it was argued that although the Scottish economy was weak, any severance of the ties with England would lead to the economic abyss. According to Lord McClay:

Without a doubt Scotland has benefited most from the Union and anything in the way of a severance from England would almost certainly spell disaster. The setting up a separate Scottish Parliament would certainly result in the removal to England of many Scottish industries and merchant traders and others on whom even today Scotland is losing hold.[52]

A Scottish parliament, it was argued by John Buchan, would only make the situation worse:

Real as the needs are, to attempt to meet them by creating an elaborate legislature would be more than those needs require. Such a top heavy structure would not cure Scotland's ills; it would intensify them. It would create artificial differences, hinder co-operation and engender friction.[53]

Others argued that the creation of a Scottish parliament would lead to the emergence of an 'insidious' Irish influence on Scottish politics.[54] Although fears of Irish immigration were greatly exaggerated, most notably by the Church of Scotland, and in spite of the official refutation by the Scottish Office, many people believed that the size of the Scoto-Irish Catholic community was much greater than it actually was.[55] Horne argued that the 'Irish' community would act as a cohesive block and end up as a controlling influence on any Scottish parliament. Furthermore, a belief that this community was increasing both through higher birth rates and immigration led John Buchan to conclude that one in every five Scottish children now being born was 'Irish Catholic'.[56] In short, the Scottish community was not cohesive enough to be an independent polity.

Unionist politicians veered uneasily between promoting economic arguments against home rule to ones which encouraged dependency. Unionism underwent a radical shift in emphasis in the thirties. The notion that the Union was an equal partnership between Scotland and England was replaced with the argument that Scotland needed England to survive. According to Sir Reginald Macleod of Macleod: 'Let Scotland not by yielding to some fancied enthusiasm expose herself to the material loss which I feel sure would occur if she had her own parliament'.[57] After all, it was claimed 'Scotland looks south for her markets'.[58]   This highly negative and defeatist view of the Anglo Scottish relationship reached its apotheosis with the claim made by Sir Robert Horne that:

The Welsh are showing the kind of wisdom that is generally attributed to the Scot, because, knowing that the amount of their unemployment is so much greater than elsewhere, probably they realise that they would find great difficulty in providing unemployment benefit by themselves, and they are wiser to rely on the richer country than to seek separation.[59]

The contrast between this statement and the pre-war espousal of Unionism could not have been greater. It was hardly a confident endorsement of the Union. Others lined up to put the boot into Scottish national self-esteem and reinforce the message of Scottish dependency. Not only were the Scots materially indebted to the English, they relied on the beneficence of their southern neighbours for civilisation itself. According to Robert Boothby:

> Prior to 1707, the Scottish people were a pack of miserable savages, living in incredible poverty and squalor, and playing no part in the development of civilisation. Since 1707, they have been partners in the greatest undertaking the world has ever seen. It was the Union that turned the Scots into an imperial race.[60]

Walter Elliot claimed that the Scots had no tradition of parliamentary government to fall back on and, unlike England, Scotland's tradition and values were centred around the Kirk and this was a 'heritage of nomination and not of democracy'.[61] As others pointed out, the Scots were good at governing others, but not themselves: 'It is not merely a case of being able to govern themselves. We think we are fit to govern all the world. Are they (home rulers) willing to shut out Scotsmen and Scotswomen from taking the biggest positions?'[62] For some the nation was to fractious and divided for self-government. As Sir John Cargil told readers of the *Scotsman* 'Could they imagine what a Scottish parliament would be like? He could and would not like to dwell on it'.[63] Unable to address the problems of economic structural imbalance which were believed to be the cause of growing nationalist sentiment, Unionists increasingly retreated into negative arguments based on Scottish dependency.

This argument, however, sat uneasily with the appeal to the past achievements of Scotland in the Union. Furthermore, it was a highly emotional and sentimental vision of past Scottish grandeur. According to Bob Boothby, the 'parrot cry' of Scottish home rule was nothing compared to 'our phenomenal control of a world-wide Empire that has made the name of Scotland famous, admired and respected in every quarter of the globe.'[64] His claims that the Scots still remained and 'iron race', despite the recent economic disasters chimed in with other Unionist propaganda which claimed that it was Scottish resilience in the face of adversity which was one of the key defining national characteristics. The Glasgow Empire Exhibition of 1938 was an attempt to marry memories of previous Scottish grandeur with economic opportunity. The appointment of John Buchan as Canadian Colonial Governor General was likewise hyped as another example of Scottish achievement. Unionist election manifestos still carried the Edwardian battle cry that 'nothing will detract from the fine worth and importance of that wider and noble imperial patriotism to which Scotsmen have never been indifferent'.[65] Yet, few could escape from the internal contradictions contained within the Unionist message. On the one hand, it was claimed that the Scots were dependent on England and could not govern themselves. On the other, it was claimed that Scotsmen were instrumental in the running of the British Empire and that traditional qualities such as ambition, independence, hard headedness and entrepreneurship were still to be found in abundance and that 'the prestige and reputation of our race are as high and as great as they ever were'.[66]

Unionism had to tread a fine line of acknowledging Scottish national sentiment and its grievances without promoting political nationalism. Safe ways had to be found of reinforcing the idea of Scottish nationality which would not escalate into greater demands for home rule. Indeed, although much of Scottish national sentiment was believed to come from a feeling that Scotland was not being treated fairly and that her nationality was in danger of slipping into a mere province of England, it was argued that the legitimisation of this identity would not only dissipate this sense of unease, but would also diffuse the threat of nationalism. By appealing to the Scottish sense of nationhood, it was believed in Unionist circles, that Scottish national sentiment could be appeased. According to John Buchan there had to be some tinkering with the system in order to satisfy 'a legitimate national pride and to intensify that consciousness of individuality and idiom which is what is meant, or what I mean, by national spirit'.[67]

Among the various proposals put forward were; the restoration of Hollyrood palace as a royal residence, more visits from the royal family, the relocation of the Scottish Secretary of State and the Scottish Office to Edinburgh and 'a clear Scottish policy'.[68] Given the lack of resources at the disposal of the Scottish Office, it could do little more than scratch the surface of the economic problems. The Hillington industrial park, the various commissions and enquiries into economic problems and the Empire Exhibition did little to diversify the economy or create new jobs, Yet, an important element in Unionist thinking was the idea that it was important to be seen to be doing something. Consequently, gesture was substituted for substance. High profile projects such as the Empire Exhibition and the setting up of the Scottish Office had an important element of propaganda value attached to them. The Scottish Office was to be a visible sign of Scottish national identity, although the decision to award the design to an English architect brought howls of protests and undid much of propaganda value.[69]

Administrative devolution, as outlined in the Gilmour Report, was a twin strategy designed to appeal to Scottish sentiment, while at the same time counteract demands for Scottish home rule. It was argued that what Scotland needed was not more government, but better government. By streamlining and consolidating the administration of Scotland into the Scottish Office and relocating it to Edinburgh, it was believed that this would bring the government closer to the people. Administrative devolution would counteract the claims that government in London was too remote and not up to speed with the peculiarities of Scotland. After all, the remit of the Scottish Office would be to take decisions on Scotland in Scotland by Scotsmen. All in all, it was claimed that this would make government more visible, more efficient and more accountable. In the rhetoric of Unionist politicians, it would allow the Scots to make their own decisions. Yet, there were other reasons behind the reform of the government of Scotland. There were purely practical matters to consider. The remit of the Scottish Office had grown and administratively, it left a lot to be desired. There was a practical need for greater co-ordination between departments and government boards. The role of government had been constantly expanding and had clearly outgrown its late nineteenth century seed pot. To survive it needed to be planted in new terrain. There were further concerns that the administration of the United Kingdom was too centralised and strategic fears about the effect of aerial bombing convinced many ministers that the dispersal of government agencies was a matter of national security.[70] The principle advantage of administrative devolution as a policy option, however, was that it had the appearance of delegating power to Scotland, but in actual fact control was retained at Westminster. Indeed, it is possible to argue that administrative devolution strengthened the hand of central government in Scotland.[71]

Unionist politicians, however, did not have a happy time in Scotland during the thirties. The use of gesture politics, administrative devolution and economic scare mongering were not positive policy options. Few had any illusions that these solutions simply pasted over the gaping faults in the Scottish economy. Scottish economic under-achievement was pronounced throughout the thirties and things only began to pick up in the latter years as a result of rearmament which in itself, was not enough to halt a major downturn in 1937. Privately, and often publicly, Unionist politicians denounced the policy of their own National Government. The decision to scrap the Cunard shipping programme in 1932 brought forth a passionate outburst from Walter Elliot.[72] Mining legislation was denounced by Bob Boothby as working against the interests of the Scottish industry.[73] No doubt much of this was due to a sense of frustration at the feeling of impotence in the face of problems whose magnitude was such that no solution seemed possible. The gestures and the futile attempts to instil a 'feel good' factor into Scottish public life were all very well, but according to the Scottish Secretary of State, Walter Elliot, writing in 1937:

> will not in themselves dispose of the problems upon whose solution a general improvement in Scottish social and economic conditions depends. It is the consciousness of their existence which is reflected, not in the small and unimportant Nationalist Party, but in the dissatisfaction and unease amongst moderate and reasonable people of every rank- a dissatisfaction expressed in every book written about Scotland now for several years.[74]

Until the nation was socially and economically regenerated, the underlying cause of dissatisfaction with the Union would remain and while it had not as yet crystallised into a powerful political movement, few doubted its potential. The experience of the inter-war years had seen Unionism degenerate from a powerful and confident ideology into one which was negative and defeatist. It had witnessed the triumph of a political consensus between Labour and the Unionists that Scotland was economically dependent on England. But it had also demonstrated the impotence of the Union to deal with Scotland's endemic structural failings in society and economy and, it was recognised, so long as these failings festered, there was always the potential for a nationalist upsurge. The outbreak of war in 1939, however, seemed to provide answers to all of these problems.

NOTES

[1] See I.G.C. Hutchison, *A Political History of Modern Scotland, 1832-1924*, (Edinburgh, 1986), pp. 277-333.
[2] See J. Melling, *Rent Strikes: Peoples' Struggle for Housing in West Scotland, 1890-1916*, (Edinburgh, 1983); I. McLean, *The Legend of Red Clydeside*, (Edinburgh, 1983) and C. Harvie, *No Gods and Precious Few Heroes*, (London, 1981), pp. 28-34.
[3] See Hutchison, *Political History*, pp. 309-33 and R.J. Finlay, 'Scottish Conservatism and Unionism Since 1918' in M. Francis & I. Zweiniger-Bargielowska (eds), *The Conservatives and British Society, 1880-1990*, (Cardiff, 1996), pp. 111-27.
[4] See R.H. Campbell, *The Rise and Fall of Scottish Industry*, (Edinburgh, 1980), pp. 133-64; P.L. Payne, *Growth and Contraction: Scottish Industry 1860-1990*, (Dundee, 1992), pp. 25-36 and D.H. Aldcroft, *The European Economy, 1914-1980*, (London, 1980), pp. 43-80.
[5] See R.J. Finlay, 'National Identity in Crisis: Politicians, Intellectuals and the 'End of Scotland', 1920-39', *History*, 79 (1994), pp. 242-59.

[6] See for example the pessimistic debates carried out in the *Scots Magazine*, 1926-7.

[7] Perhaps the best example of this mood is to be found in G.M. Thomson, *Caledonia: or the Future of the Scots*, (London, 1927).

[8] Mitchell Library, Glasgow, Muirhead Mss., Robert Munro to R.E. Muirhead, 11 Jan. 1922.

[9] James Kidd (Unionist Member for Springburn), *H.C. Debs.*, vol. 127, col. 2044, 16 April 1920.

[10] *ibid.,* col. 2059.

[11] *Self-Determination for Scotland*, (Glasgow, 1919), p. 5.

[12] *Scottish Home Rule*, June 1922, p.30.

[13] *Self-Determination for Scotland*, pp. 9-10.

[14] James Kidd, *H.C. Debs.* vol. 127, col. 2045, 16 April 1920.

[15] *Self-Determination for Scotland*, p. 5.

[16] *Scotsman,* 10 May 1924.

[17] NLS, Acc. 3721, MacDonald to Muirhead, 11 Jan. 1924.

[18] *Scottish Home Rule,* April 1924, pp. 89-90.

[19] F.M. Leventhal, *Arthur Henderson*, (Manchester, 1989).

[20] For example, see Winston Churchill's introduction to David Kirkwood's autobiography, *My Life of Revolt*, (London, 1924).

[21] Michael Keating and David Bleiman, *Labour and Scottish Nationalism*, (London, 1979), pp. 98-101.

[22] David Howell, *A Lost Left: Three Studies in Socialism and Nationalism*, (Manchester, 1986), pp. 229-65.

[23] See Thomson, *Caledonia*, pp. 18-23.

[24] See Finlay, 'National Identity in Crisis'.

[25] NLS, Acc. 6058, Box 1, Maxton to R. Scott, 2 May 1928.

[26] T. Johnston, *Memories*, (London, 1952), p.66.

[27] *Daily Record*, 9 Jan. 1929.

[28] *STUC Annual Report 1931.*

[29] *Scotsman*, 27 Jan. 1933.

[30] See Finlay, 'Pressure Group or Political Party'.

[31] Edinburgh Divisional Council ILP, Memorandum, Aug. 1931.

[32] *Scotsman*, 13 Feb. 1932.

[33] NLS, Acc. 3721, Box 81, undated memo.

[34] *H.C. Debs.*, vol. 272, col. 292. 22 Nov. 1932.

[35] *ibid.,* col. 307.

[36] *Daily Record*, 23 Oct. 1931.

[37] *Glasgow Chamber of Commerce Journal*, Sep. 1927.

[38] *ibid.,* Sep. 1933.

[39] *Edinburgh Evening News,* May 1931.

[40] *Glasgow Evening Citizin,* 14 Oct. 1931.

[41] *H.C. Debs.,* vol 272, col. 238, 22 Nov. 1932.

[42] *ibid.,* col. 293.

[43] *ibid.,* col. 301.

[44] See Finlay, 'National Identity in Crisis'.

[45] *H.C. Debs.,* vol. 272, col. 262, 22 Nov. 1932.

[46] See R.J. Finlay, *Independent and Free: Scottish Politics and the Origins of the Scottish National Party, 1918-1945,* (Edinburgh, 1994), pp. 91-3.

[47] *Scotsman,* 25 Nov. 1932.

[48] NLS, Acc. 7295, 'Anti nationalist Propaganda'.

[49] Campbell, *Rise and Fall of Scottish Industry,* pp. 133-64.

[50] *H.C. Debs.,* vol. 272, col. 238, 22 Nov. 1932.

[51] *ibid.*

[52] Lord Maclay, *Times,* 15 Nov. 1932.

[53] *H.C. Debs.,* vol 272, col. 261.

[54] *ibid.,* col. 245.

[55] See S.J. Brown, 'Outside the Covenant: The Scottish Presbyterian Churches and Irish Immigration, 1922-38', *Innes Review,* XLIII (1991), pp. 19-46.

[56] *H.C. Debs.,* vol. 272, col. 261, 22 Nov. 1932.

[57] *Daily Record,* 26 Nov. 1932.

[58] *Morning Post,* 19 Nov. 1932.

[59] *H.C. Debs.,* vol. 272, col. 341, 22 Nov. 1932.

[60] *The Nation,* 9 March 1932.

[61] Walter Elliot, The Scottish Heritage in Politics' in the duke of Atholl and others, *A Scotsman's Heritage,* (London, 1932), pp. 64-5.

[62] *H.C. Debs.,* vol 272, col. 304, 24 Nov. 1932.

[63] *Scotsman,* 29 June 1934.

[64] *Scots Independent,* Jan. 1930, p.120.

[65] *The Campaign Guide 1935.*

[66] *H.C. Debs.,* vol. 272, col. 238, 22 Nov 1932.

[67] *Ibid.,* col. 262.

[68] See Finlay, 'National Identity in Crisis'.

[69] *ibid.*

[70] See James Mitchell, *Conservatives and the Union: A Survey of Conservative Party Attitudes to Scotland,* (Edinburgh, 1990), pp. 17-26.

[71] See R.J. Finlay, 'In Defence of Oligarchy: Scotland in the Twentieth Century', *Scottish Historical Review,* 196 (1994), pp. 103-12.

[72] *Daily Record*, 12 Feb. 1932.
[73] *Glasgow Herald*, 20 June 1931.
[74] Quoted in R.H. Campbell, 'The Economic Case for Nationalism: Scotland', in R. Mitchison (ed), *The Roots of Nationalism: Studies in Northern Europe*, (Edinburgh, 1980), p. 151.

CHAPTER FIVE

Devolution or Centralism: The Second World War and Scottish Politics

The extent to which the Second World War marked a radical turning point in the development of British politics is still a major source of contention among historians.[1] For many, the war was the principle catalyst in the formation of the consensus politics of the post-war era in which the state took upon itself the responsibility of ensuring that it provided a minimum standard of social well being for all citizens.[2] The triumph of corparatist values, state welfarism and demand management economics, can all be said to owe their origins to the experience of total war in the years from 1939 to 1945 in which government, desperate to mobilise the maximum resources for the war effort, formed a tacit agreement with the people that the experience of mass unemployment and social dislocation in the inter-war years would never be repeated.[3] Propaganda emphasised that the war was not only being fought to defeat Fascism in Europe and Japanese militarism in the East, but was also about reconstructing a 'new' Britain, where much of the inequality and unfairness of the inter-war period would be swept away and a new social order established.[4] The government did much to promote the notions that everybody was doing their bit and that the nation was pulling together in a common cause, although the reality of the war experience demonstrates quite clearly that class divisions and tensions remained firmly entrenched.[5] In any case, no matter what the reality, such images of cooperation and the nation working together for a greater good had a profound effect in shaping and reinforcing British political idealism.

The war was also important because it fully demonstrated the capabilities of the British state. The war vindicated those who had argued in the inter-war era that government ought to mobilise more of the nation's resources to combat unemployment and social deprivation, while shaming those who had pessimistically wrung their hands and claimed that government was powerless in the face of international economic forces. During the war, the state pervaded every aspect of life. It told you where to work and what to make, what to buy, where to go and what to eat. The war illustrated what could be done if the political will was there.[6] This political will was fed by the Beveridge Report, which was published in 1942 and laid down the blueprint for post-war British social reconstruction. The state would no longer stand by and idly claim its impotence. The state was now expected to lead in peacetime, as in wartime, from the front and conquer those evils of poverty, sloth, want, ignorance and idleness which were for some just as big a threat to British society as the Nazi invasion. As Scottish society had suffered disproportionally from such evils in the inter-war period, it should come as no surprise that the wartime change in British ideology should have had a greater resonance north of the border.

The Road to Devolution?

The war was greeted with grim acceptance in Scottish political circles, although it did put the SNP in a quandary. Firstly, the party had endorsed a policy of non-conscription until a Scottish parliament had been created. Secondly, it put the brakes on MacCormick's proposed Scottish Convention which had its first meeting of September 1939 cancelled due to the outbreak of war. MacCormick was hopeful that this delay would be temporary, but was acutely conscious that the party's policy of non-conscription would frighten away potential support, if not engender open hostility. Other moderates within the party also began to question their bravado of 1937: 'It would be posible for nationalists, no doubt, to run their heads into the noose, and get themselves thrown into prison or put before a firing squad... but would that be of much avail after the war, when the time comes to resume....?'[7] Although the party chairman, Andrew Dewar Gibb, still claimed that there was a chance of some last minute reconciliation between Germany and Britain, most were aware that the chance for peace was lost and that the policy of non-conscription would bring the party into disrepute. Few believed that it was a sensible option and argued that should it be implemented, then the SNP would be tarred with the brush of unpatriotic behaviour and lose what little credibility remained. This feeling was further compounded when it was revealed that party members were receiving unsolicited German propaganda via the Italian embassy.[8] The leadership struggled to make up its mind. It was conscious that the party could split irrevocably over the issue. The hierarchy was compelled to act and instructed all members to cooperate fully in the war effort to defend the country:

> Scotland and the Scottish people are in ever present danger from without. We see no alternative to resolute defence. Our country must be protected with all the means at our disposal ... we are unflinching in our determination to assist with all means in our power toward the defeat of Nazi Germany.[9]

While simultaniously urging Scots to do their bit for the war effort, the leadership also claimed that it would support those who would not allow themselves to be conscripted for political reasons.[10] It was a mish mash of a policy with no clear direction and was designed to try and hold together an increasingly disparate and divided party.

MacCormick had been encouraged in the late thirties by sympathetic noises emanating from Labour and Liberal circles in favour of Scottish home rule. He believed that the party's exclusive and sectarian approach in the past had isolated sympathetic elements in the British political mainstream. In any case, the SNP's electoral strategy had failed to deliver any dividends. The Liberal Party had always maintained some formal commitment to Scottish home rule and there were significant links between the parties throughout the thirties, mainly in the form of people who held dual membership. Labour had blown hot and cold on the issue of a Scottish parliament, although after 1936, especially when it became apparent that the SNP had passed its electoral high water mark, it blew decidedly warmer. A recognition that not only had Scotland suffered disproportionally during the depression, but also that the nation was not emerging from it as quickly as England, had led some politicians to reassess the need for a Scottish parliament. In the words of Tom Johnston in 1936: 'Scotland must have a legislative Assembly of its own, to deal with its own special grievances and own special needs.'[11] The focal point of Labour's reassessment was the London Scots Self-Government Committee which was formed in 1937.[12] It comprised of Johnston as President, James Barr as Chairman, Thomas Burns, Norrie Fraser and Alex MacLaren as officios and among others it its ranks were; Robert Gibson, J.R. Leslie, Andrew MacLaren, Neil MacLean, Malcolm

MacMillan. L. MacNeil Weir, George Mathers, Naomi Mitchison and J.C. Welsh. In short, it contained many of the leading lights in the Scottish Parliamentary Labour Party.

Underlying the Committee's commitment to a Scottish parliament was its analysis of the Scottish economy which, it was argued, was over-dependent on the traditional heavy industries: 'Modern Scotland, with her crazy ill balance of industry, 40% of her productive workers and probably half her capital, still locked up in the over-developed 'heavy' and export industries.'[13] It was argued that the attempts by the National Government and the Scottish business community to diversify into other sectors had failed and that socialist planning was necessary to rectify Scotland's long-term structural problems. Johnston and Burns were especially critical of the Scottish Office and the lack of democratic control that the Scottish electors exercised over it. It was claimed that the Scottish Office bureaucracy was self-seeking, inefficient and prone to look after the interests of the heavy industrialists who were in league with their Conservative allies.[14] Although the Committee's ideas were not enshrined as Labour policy, they were propounded as the basis for future discussion. Support was forthcoming from the leadership which argued that Britain was over-centralised and that too many resources were concentrated in the South.[15] While Johnston and others argued that a Scottish parliament would, within the context of a federal system of British government, implement a thorough going system of economic reform, a salient aspect of their proposals was to democratise the Scottish system of government which was described as a 'rotten burgh'.[16] Not all of this was due to altruistic reasons. Scottish Labour MPs had watched with alarm the gradual increase in the number of powers which the Scottish Secretary of State had accumulated during the nineteen thirties. While this was justified by the government as part of its campaign of increasing administrative devolution, Labour politicians were worried that these powers were increasingly concentrated in the hands of one individual and not open to public scrutiny. A key part of Johnston's argument for beefing up the Scottish Grand Committee was to scrutinise the activities of the Scottish Office.[17] Furthermore, as Labour was frozen out of the political system for the foreseeable future, there was a concern that Scottish public policy was being dictated by the interests of a narrow group of Conservatives and their heavy industrialist allies. Indeed, Scottish Labour claimed that the key problems in Scottish society and economy were due to problems associated with the power of dictitorial industrialists: 'Scotland has indeed been ruthlessly exploited and bled white, not by England, but by her own industrialists.'[18] Support for a Scottish parliament was mooted as a way to check the power of Scottish capital and government administration.

All this was music to MacCormick's ears. Labour attitudes had also been softened by the activities of the socialist wing of the SNP. Oliver Brown, Archie Lamont and Roland Muirhead, had all engaged in debate with members of the Labour Party and had contributed to the discussion of, among other things, the nature of capitalism in Scotland and the future of the British Empire.[19] The SNP leadership had another weapon up its sleeve. The outbreak of hostilities had occasioned an electoral truce between the main parties. The SNP, however, was considered too insignificant to bother with and had been left out of the deal. It left the door open for a policy of by election intervention which, it was argued, could pay off dividends if exploited skilfully. The first opportunity to test this came with the Argyll by election in April 1940. MacCormick played his options quite skilfully. The SNP intervention was not represented as a return to a full blown electoral strategy, but as an anti-government ploy as the seat had been held by a Conservative. The Nationalists even received tacit support from some Liberal and Labour sources. Emrys Hughes, the editor of *Forward*, argued that a good socialist such as Oliver Brown should stand and some secret negotiations went on between MacCormick and the Liberal hierarchy to run John Bannerman as an independent nationalist, although it was thought that his Liberal credentials were too well known which would give rise to accusations of foul play.[20] The SNP settled on William Power, a Moderate, who was a respected journalist, anti-fascist and strong proponent of the war effort. Brown's activities in the peace movement had made him suspect in the eyes of the leadership.

Power, as the principal opposition candidate, was in a strong position from the outset. The government's inactivity and handling of the war effort was denounced, as was Conservative opposition to Scottish home rule:

> Who is not against us is for us. There is but one party in Scotland avowedly anti-national and militantly pro Union. We must sweep that party out of power in our constituencies. We must take the lead, we must rally the enemies of reaction, we must achieve that unity of radical thought and purpose which of itself alone will end the reign of Toryism in Scotland.[21]

Power won over 7,000 votes against the Conservative tally of 12,000 which clearly made it the best nationalist electoral performance to date. Power picked up the Labour and Liberal vote and the SNP campaign was more effective than the Conservative opposition which was adversely effected by the wartime call-up.[22] While the strong SNP performance was no doubt due to the government's unpopularity, it did raise the spectre of unwelcome nationalist interventions in by elections and this was could be used to put pressure on the Labour Party. MacCormick and the leadership went further in their efforts to make the SNP more acceptable to the Liberal and Labour parties. The party's pro-war stance was hardened, especially after the ending of the Phoney War. Members were urged to look out for fifth columnists and contribute to local defence schemes. The Churchill Coalition was given endorsement and support and anti-war and anti-conscriptionist organisations were hounded out of the party.[23]

In September 1940, John Taylor, the Scottish Secretary of the Labour Party, outlined proposals for the establishment of a Scottish parliament after the war.[24] MacCormick responded warmly to such plans and suggested that a united Scottish Front should be set up to promote the self-government cause.[25] It was believed in nationalist circles that the Scottish trade unions were once again hostile to English encroachments and this would provide a firm basis of support.[26] It was proposed that the organisation would blend plans for self-government with post-war reconstruction. To give it authority, it was argued that it should be as genuinely representative of Scottish society as possible:

Scotsmen and Scotswomen preparing for the attack on post-war problems ... composed of representatives from Scottish industrial, political and cultural bodies throughout Scotland, so that there may be in being a purely Scottish representative body which and will act in Scottish interests.[27]

As a starting point, the organisation would push for a Scottish plebiscite at the end of the war on Scottish home rule. MacCormick also made approaches to Lady Glen Coats of the Scottish Liberal Party and was assured of support.[28] Furthermore, it was made known that the SNP would refrain from contesting elections if official candidates were prepared to endorse a post-war plebiscite on Scottish home rule.[29] By the beginning of 1941 Taylor had intimated to the nationalists that their proposals had been accepted in principle and that they could count on the support of the Scottish Labour Party. Promises were also made that Labour's London leadership would not interfere in the project. Plans were laid that each of the parties would send three delegates to a special meeting.[30]

MacCormick was buoyed up by the fact that Thomas Johnston had been appointed Scottish Secretary of State by Churchill in February 1941 and that there was now a pro-home ruler in a position of considerable influence. Also, there was an imminent Dumbartonshire by election which enabled the nationalists put pressure on Labour by threatening an SNP intervention. Johnston, in particular, could well remember that it was a nationalist candidate in 1932 who had cost him the seat and much of Labour's conciliatory stance of home rule at this time was designed to stop an SNP candidate standing. MacCormick used the opportunity to push through his idea of a united front and he was determined that Labour would fall into line:

The Council of the Scottish National Party in considering its attitude to the Dunbartonshire election, had before it a friendly reply from the Labour Party in response to its recent approaches. It was decided, however, to seek further assurances before a final decision was reached.[31]

To reinforce the message the nationalists went ahead and selected a candidate, although Labour hurriedly agreed to a meeting in which the necessary reassurances were given about the party's commitment to a Scottish parliament.[32] It was a small price to pay to avoid what could have been a potentially embarrassing and troublesome intervention.

Other indications were available to show that Labour was taking the issue more seriously. In July 1941 Johnston stated publicly that he was prepared to support devolution because of the lack of time devoted to Scottish affairs in Westminster.[33] Many nationalists were won over by the new Scottish Secretary's deft handling of Scottish issues in London and his ability to redress numerous grievances. Meetings of the Scottish Grand Committee were moved to Edinburgh where more time and attention was devoted to Scottish issues and in December 1941 the Scottish Council of the Labour Party voted by seventy one votes to thirty five that:

> Whatever the exact powers of our new legislature, we are mostly agreed that a Scottish parliament elected by the Scottish people would be the best instrument for the efficient government of this country.[34]

Although home rule had its critics in the Labour Party, most notably Emmanuel Shinwell and Pat Dollan, it appeared to many that the issue was undergoing a revival. Labour's plans for post-war reconstruction, while not definitely proposing a Scottish parliament, were committed to some form of devolution. MacCormick pressed Taylor on this and was assured that this was the most likely option. The plans for a cross party convention looked promising and MacCormick was confident that there was enough common ground between the nationalists, Liberals and Labour to form the basis of a united campaign and home rule proposal.[35]

MacCormick's united front campaign, however, was not universally supported by the rank and file of the SNP. One obvious danger with the policy of a united front was that it neglected normal party activities in favour of secret meetings and dealings with other political leaders. This conspiratorial approach to party politics excluded ordinary members from participating in the process. Furthermore, until the process of negotiation with the other parties was completed, SNP activity was forced into a kind of stasis. Unlike the established parties, the SNP organisation was fragile and did not have the members of parliament or elected local councillors who could give the party some form of stability during the war years. Indeed, the message coming from the hierarchy was that political survival should be the sole objective of the party for the duration of the war.[36] It was hardly likely to inspire. Discontent came from two sources. Firstly, there were those who had adhered to the anti-conscription stance and demanded support and endorsement from the party. More often than not, this group was drawn from the radical wing and their actions deeply embarrassed the hierarchy. Secondly, there were those who were committed to the belief that the SNP should function as an independent political party. This meant contesting elections, formulating policy and challenging the other parties. MacCormick's strategy had relegated such activity in favour of the Convention approach. Favourable noises from Labour on the issue of Scottish home rule was enough to keep such discontent in check. Yet, as MacCormick's policy began to run into the sands, such divisions within the SNP became more and more pronounced.

The party's credibility was badly damaged in December 1941 when it became apparent that the SNP did not have the resources to mount a campaign in the Edinburgh Central by election against an official Tory candidate. Radicals blamed the leadership for this state of affairs and complained bitterly that MaCormick's obsession with courting Liberal and Labour favour had been at the expense of the good of the party.[37] Inadequate finances, a dilapidated organisation and poor morale were all cited a reasons for the failure to put up a candidate. Furthermore, it was claimed that a the candidate was a Conservative, a nationalist intervention would not have damaged the SNP's prospects of forming a united front with the Liberals and Labour. What was worse, in the eyes of the radicals, was such a public admission of the SNP's weakness which damaged the party's credibility. Further trouble was in store for the leadership in the early years of 1942. Firstly, there was the public trial of Douglas Young for his anti-conscription stance. This generated an enormous amount of publicity which the leadership believed undermined the party's credibility. It damaged the party's pro-war stance and revealed the extent of division within the ranks. Also,

Young acted as a very public focal point around which the discounted radicals could rally. Young became a cause célèbre and his action considerably buoyed up the radicals who believed that the time was now ripe for the party to move in a different direction.[38] The second major difficulty facing the leadership was the Cathcart by election in April 1942. The pro leadership candidate, William Whyte, was one of the party's most vociferous supporters of the war effort. In his own words: 'I therefore pledge myself to give general support to such a government (the Coalition) ... I should state that I have the utmost confidence in Mr Thomas Johnston and will endeavour to give him every support'.[39] Also, to confuse the situation, he chose to stand as an independent nationalist, rather than fly the official SNP banner. Whyte's campaign was conducted on familiar lines. The Conservatives were denounced as the only party against home rule and Whyte was more than fulsome in his praise for the efforts of Tom Johnston.

The campaign was a disaster. Radicals chose not to support Whyte because of his pro-war stance and the party was left without an organisation to run an effective campaign. The trail of Young overshadowed the election and the press picked up on the nationalist anti-conscription message which was at complete variance with what Whyte and MacCormick were trying to portray in Cathcart. Also, there were other more able candidates standing against the official Conservative and unlike the Argyll by-election in 1940, the nationalists did not have a monopoly of the opposition vote. Whyte came bottom of the poll with five and a half per cent of the vote. Each section of the party interpreted the outcome according to their own sensibilities. As far as the leadership was concerned, the fault lay with the adverse publicity generated by the radicals and the trial of Douglas Young. According to MacCormick, the cause of Scottish home rule would never make any progress so long as the public identified Scottish nationalism with the activities of irresponsible radicals. As a counter blast, radicals contrasted the amount of publicity Young's trial generated compared to the efforts of Whyte. Also, the timid approach of the leadership had failed to mobilise any support in the election. Both sides believed that their actions were vindicated by the outcome and both were baying for blood when the party met for its annual conference in the summer of 1942.

The Rise of Centralism

MacCormick's strategy had also began to run into difficulties with the Labour Party. Johnston revolutionised the nature of Scottish government during the war years. As a Secretary of State, Johnston was remarkably efficient at demanding and getting more powers and concessions from Westminster.[40]   One of the key grievances in Scotland was that new industry continued to be located in the south while Scotland was used primarily for storage. Johnston started to reverse this trend and his policy of the 'strongman in the Cabinet' showed that the current system could deliver benefits to Scotland if it was operated effectively. This contradicted many of the notions of the home rule movement that the system was beyond repair and would not work to Scotland's advantage. Johnston initiated a new type of approach to political management. The complaint of the thirties was that the too much power resided in the hands of Scottish Secretary and that government in Scotland was unaccountable. Johnston freed this up by employing consensus type policies. Trade unions and business were invited to contribute to ideas of post-war reconstruction. Also, he set up the office of the Ex-Secretaries of State for Scotland, which comprised of all those still living who had once held this office. It was designed to bring experience, talent and clout to plans for post-war reconstruction.[41] Furthermore, it was to ensure that policy would have cross party support. Again, Johnston had circumvented one of the key claims of the home rule movement that a Scottish parliament was necessary to ensure that the government of Scotland was more representative and accountable. Yet, the critical point was that such policies and such government worked and was seen to work. Claims that the Union had passed its sell by date and that it was no longer effective were not borne out by the experience of Johnston's wartime administration.

The SNP annual conference of 1942 was arguably the most dramatic turning point in the party's history. With each side in combative mood and determined to take no prisoners, the radicals proposed Douglas Young as Chairman in opposition to William Power. This was a direct challenge to the moderates as Young was the very epitome of what

MacCormick had been trying to eradicate from the nationalist ranks. The vote was a narrow one, with Young winning by thirty three votes to twenty nine. In itself, the rejection of Power in favour of Young was not necessarily an endorsement of the anti-conscription line. Many used Young's candidature as a way of impressing upon the leadership that they were unsatisfied with the party's progress.[42] Also, Power was old and lacked vision. Although the meeting had been acrimonious, it was no more so than others in the past. Furthermore, given the fractious nature of the SNP and its tendency to degenerate into semi autonomous units each pushing their own preferred strategy and campaign, the election of Young was by no means a clear signal for ending MacCormick's convention policy. Yet, MacCormick could not accept such a public rejection and left the party taking half the delegates with him, although many were subsequently to return when it became apparent that the SNP was not going to transform itself into a republican anti-conscription movement. A salient reason for MacCormick's abrupt secession many have been that in his eyes such a public endorsement of an anti-conscriptionist candidate may have put the nationalists beyond the pale of respectable politics and rendered co-operation with Labour and the Liberals impossible.

Whatever the reason, MacCormick's aspirations to create a united front were evaporating. Johnston's consensual approach to wartime Scottish politics meant offering places to all within the Scottish political establishment. The SNP had conspicuously failed to prove that it had a power base in Scottish society and it was questionable if it represented the views of anybody other than a vocal tiny minority. Furthermore, Johnston's inclusion of Conservatives into the various committees of reconstruction and quangos, together with the roles of Elliot, Gilmour and others in the Ex-Secretaries of State Committee, meant that the SNP's policy of unremitting hostility to the Tory Party was not likely to win friends and influence people associated with the post-war reconstruction of Scottish society. Indeed, nationalist inclusion in this process after their recent propaganda would have been very embarrassing and any hints that Labour had been colluding with a SNP anti-Conservative campaign would have undermined the whole notion of a wartime truce between the major parties. In any case, it was soon apparent that the blueprints for the post war reconstruction of Scottish society were being laid without a nationalist input as projects such as the Clyde Valley Plan appeared.[43] Also, Johnston's previous enthusiasm for home rule was beginning to cool and his response to a direct question as to whether he still supported the idea of setting up a Scottish parliament at the end of the war was decidedly ambiguous:

> I intend to make an effort to keep our country meanwhile on the map and to do my utmost - and within the limits imposed by the circumstances imposed by the circumstances in which we find ourselves - to persuade Scots and English alike that it is desirable we should be allowed to work out our own problems in our own way.[44]

Although a parliament was not dismissed, it was not directly endorsed. Johnston was a skilful politician and did not give away any more than was needed. Aware of the frisive nature of Scottish nationalism, he was not prepared to give ammunition to the SNP, nor was he going to allow himself to be held hostage to a direct commitment. It was enough for many in the SNP who set to work attacking both Johnston's wartime regime and Labour's failure to give an unequivocal commitment to Scottish home rule:

> No doubt the setting up of such committees and advisory councils may be quite satisfying to the Quislings and capitalist imperialists in Scotland as well as the bureaucrats in London... why the present day followers of Keir Hardie have allowed themselves to be diddled by those Scots and English capitalists and imperialists who are quite pleased when Scottish socialists call for international socialism knowing full well that so long as Scots citizens allow themselves to be fobbed off with an ideal slogan, instead of insisting on the first practical step towards the ideal state, namely self-government, all will be well for capitalist imperialism.[45]

Radicals increasingly attacked Labour from a socialist perspective and sought to capitalise on Scottish wartime grievances. There would be no compromise with Johnston's wartime government.

The nationalist movement after 1942 was divided into two camps; a radical group committed to the idea of maintaining the SNP as an independent party and a moderate group which was committed to using pressure group tactics to influence other political parties. Although such divisions appeared deep and irreconcilable, the fact of the matter was that both groups had a large body of support which had a foot in both camps.[46] Indeed, much of the subsequent development of nationalist politics in the period up to the early fifties was a competition to see which strategy would be vindicated. The SNP set to work to reconstitute itself as an independent political party under the leadership of Arthur Donaldson and Dr Robert McIntyre.[47] The laxity of the previous decade was not to be repeated and discipline was strengthened. Membership of other political parties was forbidden, social and economic policies were laid out, the constitutional objective was defined as independence, an electoral strategy was formulated and the organisational infrastuture was built up. It was, in many ways, a return to the principles of the National Party of Scotland. Although the process of regeneration was an arduous one, by the time of the annual conference in 1943 most members noted a difference and the party had a greater membership and greater degree of unity than at any time in recent history.[48] Some problems, did remain, however. The party chairman, Douglas Young, although a radical, was not committed to independence, nor did he fully endorse a policy of seeking a mandate by contesting elections. Paradoxically, his strategy and objectives were closer to MacCormick's. However, as a guest of His Majesty in prison for his refusal to be conscripted, McIntyre and Donaldson were allowed to carry on building up the party in their direction without any interference.

The Kirkcaldy by election of early 1944 vindicated the direction the party was taking. Donaldson as party agent, had a difficult job in controlling Douglas Young as the candidate, although this was in fact achieved. The official candidate was Labour and a nationalist intervention put paid to any notion that the SNP would be part of a cross party or united front campaign. McIntryre's membership drive and organisational reforms had paid off and the SNP was able to mount an effective campaign, which by all accounts was more successful than their opponents.[49] Furthermore, Young's manifesto displayed greater political acumen than previous nationalist campaigns. Female conscription and deportation to factories in England was denounced and was a marked feature of the attack on the government's wartime record. This was an issue which raised many hackles in Scotland and had been denounced by the trade union movement The poor rate of Scottish allocation of new industry was another key issue and Young campaigned on a leftist platform of greater social reform. It paid off dividends and Young was beaten by just a couple of thousand votes and he succeeded in pushing the Christian socialist into third place. It was taken as evidence that a well organised and committed national party with a clear sense of direction could make an electoral impact. The same formula was used again in April 1945 at the by election in Motherwell when Robert McIntyre was the first member of the SNP to be elected to Parliament. It was a great moral booster and although the seat was lost a number of weeks later in the general election, it was viewed by members as the party's greatest success to date. For McIntyre and others, this was the only viable strategy and it was enshrined in the SNP constitution of 1947. The success of the SNP in these two by elections was instrumental in shoring up a last ditch commitment by Labour and in the general election of 1945, the creation of a Scottish parliament was deemed the second priority after the defeat of Japan. Yet, the experience of wartime had fundamentally compromised Labour's ability and willingness to deliver.

NOTES

[1] See K. Morgan, *The People's Peace: British History, 1945-1990*, (Oxford, 1990), pp. 3-29; P. Addison, *The Road to 1945*, (London, 1975); C. Barnett, *The Audit of War: The Illusion and Reality of Britain as a Great Power*, (London, 1986).

[2] See George Peden, *British Social and Economic Policy: Lloyd George to Margaret Thatcher*, (London, 1991), pp. 118-51.

[3] Addison, *Road to 1945*; A. Calder, *The People's War*, (1975).

[4] Sian Nicholas, *The Echo of War: Home Front Propaganda and the Wartime BBC, 1939-45*, (Manchester, 1996).

[5] Morgan, *People's Peace*, pp. 3-29; A. Calder, *The Myth of the Blitz*, (London, 1991).

[6] A. Marwick, *Britain in the Century of Total War*, (London, 1968).

[7] *Scots Independent*, Oct. 1939, p.1.

[8] See R.J. Finlay, *Independent and Free: Scottish Politics and the Origins of the Scottish national party, 1918-1945*, (Edinburgh, 1994), pp. 206-10.

[9] *Scots Independent*, Oct. 1939, p.3.

[10] NLS, Young Mss, Box 44, 'Report of the Special Conference of 12 December 1939'.

[11] *Scotsman*, 23 Oct. 1936.

[12] See Thomas Burns, *Plan for Scotland*, (Perth, 1937).

[13] *ibid.*, p.9.

[14] *ibid.*

[15] C. Attlee, *The Labour Party in Perspective*, (London, 1937).

[16] Burns, *Plan for Scotland*, p.11.

[17] Johnstone's amendment to the Gilmour Report, 1937.

[18] Burns, *Plan for Scotland*, p.24.

[19] See their activities as reported in the *Scots Independent*, 1938-40.

[20] NLS, McIntyre Mss., Minute Book of the National Council of the SNP, 2 March 1940, pp. 377-78.

[21] *Scots Independent*, May 1940, p. 6.

[22] NLS, Acc. 3721, 'Press Cuttings of the Campaign in Argyll'.

[23] See Finlay, *Independent and Free*, pp. 215-17.

[24] *Scots Independent*, Sep. 1940, p. 3.

[25] *ibid.*

[26] Minute Book of the National Council of the SNP, 2 Nov. 1940, p. 415.

[27] *ibid.*, 21 Dec. 1940, p. 417.

[28] *ibid.*, 1 Feb. 1941, p. 432.

[29] *ibid.*, 21 Dec. 1940, p. 417.

[30] *ibid.*, 1 March, 1941, p. 434.

[31] *ibid.*, 1 Feb. 1941, p. 430.

[32] *ibid.*, 1 March 1941, p. 434.

[33] *Glasgow Herald*, 14 July 1941.

[34] *ibid.*, 16 Dec. 1941.

[35] *Scots Independent*, Oct, 1941, p. 1.

[36] Reports of the Organisation Secretary, Robert McIntyre, in the Minute Book of the national Council of the SNP, 1941.

[37] *ibid.*, 4 Dec. 1941.

[38] NLS, Young Mss., Box 43, Young to A.W. Donaldson, 31 March 1942.

[39] *Scots Independent*, May 1942, p. 4.

[40] G. Walker, *Thomas Johnston*, (Manchester, 1988), pp. 151-78; Chris Harvie,' Labour and Scottish Government: The Age of Tom Johnston', *The Bulletin of Scottish Politics*, (Spring 1981), pp. 1-20.

[41] R.H. Campbell, 'The Committee of Ex-Secretaries of State for Scotland and Industrial Policy, 1941-45', *Scottish Industrial History*, 2 (1981).

[42] See Finlay, *Independent and Free*, pp. 228-32.

[43] Campbell, 'Committee of Ex-Secetaries'.

[44] Nls, Acc. 3721, Box 3, Johnston to Muirhead, 29 Aug. 1942.

[45] NLS, Acc. 3721, Box 3, R.E. Muirhead to Oliver Brown, 25 May, 1942.

[46] NLS, Records of the Scottish National Convention, 1943.

[47] See Finlay, *Independent and free*, pp. 235-424.

[48] NLS, Young Mss, Box 44, 'Report of the Annual Conference of the SNP, 1943'.

[49] NLS, Acc. 3721, Box 100, 'Report of the Campaign'.

CHAPTER SIX
A New Britain?, 1945-67

British and Scottish society emerged from the Second World War with great expectations. The experience of the last war, when promises of homes for heroes came to nothing, was not going to be repeated.[1] Although the 'myth of consensus' was not as deeply implanted in the minds of the British psyche as has often been portrayed, there was, nevertheless, a mood of optimism that the state would ensure the morale and material well-being of the populace. In Scotland, such ideas had a deeper resonance than in other parts of the United Kingdom simply because there was more for the state to do in terms of economic and social regeneration. During the war, politics north of the border was dominated by the prospect of peacctime reconstruction. Johnston had initiated numerous enquires and committees to plan the social and economic regeneration of Scottish society.[2] The landslide victory for the Labour Party in the general election of 1945 confirmed this enthusiasm to build a better and fairer Britain in which the citizen, should it be necessary, would be looked after by the state from the cradle to the grave.[3] Yet, the task facing politicians in 1945 was an enormous one. The war had bankrupted the nation, there was extensive infrastructure damage caused by bombing, the international climate was deeply unsettled and the Labour government was charged with meeting high expectations with only a limited amount of resources.[4]

In Scotland, there was little disagreement on what the state needed to do. War damage compounded the problems of poor housing which had plagued Scottish society in the inter-war era. Due to a combination of wartime restrictions and avarice the private sector had not kept up with repairs and housing was deemed by most as the greatest priority facing the new government. The solution mooted by planners and experts was for a greater number of local authority houses to be built which would have cheap and affordable rents.[5] The economy, reflated in the late thirties and during the war with armament production, was over-dependent on the traditional heavy industries and desperately needed to diversify in order to avoid a repetition of the structural dislocation which had followed in the wake of the First World War. The late thirties and war years witnessed a host of publications and enquiries into the nature of the Scottish problem and politicians were well aware of the extent of the difficulties which they faced.[6] Although Labour had flirted with Scottish home rule during this period, a number of factors had emerged to render it superfluous as a policy option for post-war reconstruction. Firstly, there was the experience of the war itself. Labour's commitment to Scottish home rule in the late thirties had been conditioned by its exclusion from the growth of state power which was concentrated in the hands of the Secretary of State and his industrialist allies. The development of the corporatist state during the war had brought the Labour Party and the trade unions within the pale of the political decision making process. In any case, Labour's victory at the polls in 1945 and the revolution in political ideology during the war now made it unlikely that there would be a return to the system of the thirties where power was the prerogative of the Conservatives and their capitalist henchmen. As a means of ensuring some sort of democratic control on the government of Scotland, home rule was no longer thought to be necessary.

A second factor working against home rule as an option for post-war reconstruction was the fact that it was shown during the war that Westminster could deliver the goods. Johnston's wartime stewardship had been a success and significant concessions were wrung from the government. Factories, industrial resources, government agencies and devolved decision making had been dispatched north and for many, it now appeared that the problem in the thirties was not the system but the operation of the system. So long as the Scots continued to send spokesmen of Johnston's calibre who adhered to their own political agenda, the Union could work to the Scots' benefit. Westminster and the existing political system, it was argued, was capable of delivering what the Scots wanted, provided there was the political will and expertise to make it so.[7] A third factor militating against home rule was the overall process of British reconstruction itself. To detach or delineate Scottish reconstruction from the British process was fraught with practical difficulties and for many, this would simply delay and obstruct the pressing priorities of social and economic regeneration. The Redistribution of Industries Act of 1945 and the Town and Country Planning Act of 1947 were designed to divert new industrial production away from the prosperous areas of the south and ensure that there was a more even distribution of prosperity in the United

Kingdom. This policy had obvious appeal to the Scots.[8] The key objective of Scottish politicians was to ensure that they got as big a slice of the British cake as possible. Nationalisation, for example, was strategically conceived according to British economic priorities and planning, and a separate Scottish dimension would only confuse and complicate matters.[9] Furthermore, given the extent of Scottish structural problems, it was recognised that an indigenous reallocation of resources would not be enough.[10] More attractive was the prospect of having access to a common British pool which would be allocated on the basis of need. Again, the creation of a Scottish parliament would obstruct and complicate the process. If need was the British criteria for resource allocation, it was argued, Scotland ought to do well. For most politicians in Scotland at the end of the war, the pressing problem was the Scottish economy and social infrastructure and all other considerations would be relegated to second place. Such were the conclusions of a committee to enquire into the financial relations between Scotland and England in June 1950 which reported in July 1952.[11]

The reforms of the Labour governments of 1945-51 had a profound effect on Scottish society. The nationalisation of key industries, such as coal, transport and electricity, together with a firm commitment to the wartime strategy of economic planning, brought the British state into the lives of more Scots than at any time before. The foundation of the Welfare State brought to an end the Scottish tradition of local government boards and replaced them with new government funded agencies. The fad for planning led to the redistribution of new industry to Scotland, such as the Rolls Royce aero engines factory at Hillington, which would rectify the structural imbalance of economic reliance on shipbuilding, engineering and steel. Also, planning was designed to change the nature of the Scottish built environment with proposals for the creation of new towns which would service new industries. The provision of good, cheap, council housing was a key initiative of government designed to remove the greatest social blight in Scottish society. Health reforms and extended social provision, likewise, were designed to improve living standards in a society where the memories of the hungry thirties were still fresh. Yet, the Welfare State and the corporate economy were not created overnight in Scottish society. As was mentioned earlier, the state had a lot to do in Scotland and expectations were great, but the pressing demands on limited resources meant that some of the plans had to be sacrificed to political expediency.

The cost of the Welfare State had to be borne by increasing income from exports. The Scottish economy was in a good position to contribute due to the demands of European and Imperial reconstruction. Heavy engineering, coal, steel and shipbuilding prospered due to the destruction of the European economy and output remained high and buoyant. While it was recognised during the war that reliance on a narrow range of industries was bad for the long-term prospects of the Scottish economy, the reality of the post-war situation demanded that such concerns be put on hold in order to generate much needed export income for a cash strapped Treasury. Political expediency, likewise, dictated that the detailed planning which had been called for during the war was dropped. In any case, as far as most contemporaries were concerned, the Scottish economy looked to be in good shape. According to one leading economist, Alec Cairncross, there was no need for Scotland to get a proper share of the motor car or aircraft industries as this would simply be 'water over the damn'.[12] The demand for orders showed no signs of abating in a Europe being rebuilt on the Marshal Plan, employment prospects were good and per capita income and wages were making up ground on the losses sustained in the inter-war years. Although wages were rising in Scotland, they were still nine per cent lower than the United Kingdom average. Yet, the critical factor was that they were moving in the right direction.[13] Prophesies of doom which foretold of the dangers of over reliance on traditional heavy industries, did not seem to come to pass. Indeed, by 1958, the Scottish economy was more dependent on the heavy industries than it had been in the thirties. Given that one of the cardinal objectives of all post-war government had been to maintain full employment, politicians found, particularly by using the nationalised industries, that this could be achieved within the existing economic framework with little or no tampering. The limited resources that were available were channelled into encouraging American companies to establish themselves in Scotland and although it was soon becoming apparent that the older industries were running into problems of falling output and poor productivity, government was reluctant to either invest or aid in restructuring.[14] Yet, with full employment, good wages and improving standards of living, it did not seem to matter.

Labour lost the general election of 1951 largely because of the adverse effect of the austerity programme where, in an endeavour to restore the nation's economic fortunes, rationing was maintained and strict economic controls were enforced. As was mentioned earlier, the Welfare State in Scotland did not happen overnight. Significant problems remained in Scottish society by the time the Conservatives were returned to power in 1951. Labour's house building programme ran into difficulties. The houses built were of good quality, but used up precious resources. In 1952 a further half million were still required and more than fifty per cent of the existing stock had been built before 1900. Thirty per cent were still of two rooms or less and only twenty per cent had more than four rooms. This contrasted badly with England where less than five per cent were of two rooms or less and fifty per cent had four rooms or more.[15] The health service was still in embryonic form and only about six per cent of the total British local authority health care workers were employed in Scotland.[16]

The Conservatives won the 1951 election on a policy of consumerism and of forcing back state control. In many ways, Labour was denied justice. Having pushed through major reforms and kick started the economy into life, Labour was punished by the electorate for the experience, but the Conservatives picked up the rewards. The economy was in better shape and the controls were removed not necessarily by Conservative will power, but because the climate was now right to do so. One of the key features of Scottish political history in the fifties is the success of the Unionist Party. In the general elections between and including 1950 and 1964, the Unionists averaged forty six per cent of the vote while Labour averaged forty seven per cent. More than anything, the vagaries of the first past the post electoral system accounted for the loss and gain of seats. Political success in Scotland was dependent, as it was in the United Kingdom, on the ability of parties to present themselves as the most capable candidate for managing government. Scottish politics largely mirrored the ebb and flows of British politics. Yet a good argument can be made to claim that the Unionist party was the more successful. Indeed, Given the social structure of Scottish society with its bias in favour of the industrial working class and a smaller middle-class than the average for the rest of the United Kingdom, the Unionist vote held up remarkably well.

A number of factors can be used to explain the success of the Unionist Party in Scotland in the fifties. Firstly, there was a sense that Labour had failed to live up to expectations. The restraints of the immediate post-war years had led to shortages and the trappings of 'New Britain' could not be delivered quickly enough for most people. As we have seen, this was not the fault of the Labour Party, yet, by the early fifties, when the Conservative Party was in power, the state was in a better to position to deliver the goods. Labour's austerity programme paid off when the Conservative Party was in power, and the idea that 'you've never had it so good' was associated with the Unionist Party rather than Labour. Indeed, if we take the example of the house building boom in Scotland during the fifties it is easy to see how many associated the notion of affluence with the Conservative Party. In 1954, for example, 38, 000 new houses were constructed. Tower blocks, 'pre-fabs' and 'new towns' were the 'pragmatic' solutions offered by experts and favoured by the incoming Conservative administrations after 1951. Not only were such schemes more economical, they were the best way for the government to realise its political priority of meeting rehousing targets.

A second factor in explaining Unionist success was the party's ability to capitalise on Scottish sentiment. The Unionists berated Labour's policy of nationalisation as it meant 'de-nationalisation' for Scotland as Scottish control was moved south to London. Labour was attacked for its centralising tendencies which were associated with socialism. The Labour Party was portrayed as the party of centralism and British uniformity.[17] The Unionists advocated the notion of a partnership between England and Scotland and demanded that as much power be retained in Scotland:

> Union is not amalgamation. Scotland is a nation...... It is only since 1945, under the first socialist majority, that we have seen the policy of amalgamation superseding that of

Union. This must inevitably result from the fulfilment of the socialist creed, which is basically one of amalgamation and centralisation. To this policy we are fundamentally opposed.[18]

The Balfour Committee of 1954 recommended that as far as possible, the activities of the state in Scotland should be controlled and governed by the Scottish Office. While not conceding political devolution, the Unionist Party was keen to promote a distinctive arm of government in Scotland.[19]

Nationalist sentiment had been briefly, but ineffectively, roused in the early fifties by the Scottish National Convention (see below), the furore over Queen Elizabeth's numeral and the stealing of the Stone of Destiny. Labour was also attacked by the nationalists over its policy of nationalisation and its refusal to grant self-government.[20] At the 1948 by-election in Paisley, John MacCormick challenged the Labour candidate with Conservative and Liberal support. Such activities led to a hardening of Labour attitudes on the issue of home rule and nationalist sentiment. For example, the decision was taken in Cabinet not to return the Stone of Destiny. The Labour government recognised that a considerable body of opinion in Scotland was favourable to some form of moderate devolution, but the Cabinet could not make up its mind what to do about it. Prevarication was the order of the day and apart from an enquiry into the financial relationship between Scotland and the United Kingdom and promises to reform parliamentary procedures relating to Scottish legislation, little else was forthcoming.[21] While Labour remained stony faced, the Unionists played the Scottish card. The Saltire was flown at general elections and in combating socialism, Unionist candidates claimed to be defending Scottish national interests.[22] Any attempt to describe Scotland as a region was deemed insulting to Scottish nationhood. While most of this was mere gesture, the Unionists were able to pass themselves off as the most Scottish of the main British parties. Also, while promoting the idea of administrative devolution, Unionists never conceded anything on the principle of democratic devolution or a Scottish parliament.

Nationalist unease was present in the fifties. Disillusioned with the radicalism of the SNP and frustrated at the failure to make any nationalist or home rule electoral impact, John MacCormick organised the Scottish Convention which was designed to demonstrate popular support for moderate home rule without using the electoral machinery.[23] Aware that Scottish Labour had nominally committed itself to setting up a Scottish parliament, the Scottish Convention sought to put pressure on the Labour government to fulfil its obligations, hence MacCormick's decision to contest the Paisley by election in 1948. The decision of MacCormick to stand as a 'national' candidate in the Paisley by election with Liberal and Conservative support against Labour, did not help matters. Firstly, Labour was suspicious that home rule was being used as an anti-Labour device. Secondly, the projected home rule support did not manifest itself in the electoral outcome and Labour held the seat. The principal achievement of the by election was to raise hackles in the government and the Labour Party against the home rule campaign. In the Autumn of 1949 John MacCormick organised a petition on behalf of the Scottish Convention which collected about two million signatures in favour of Scottish home rule. The campaign was a massive undertaking and was designed to demonstrate the ground swell of popular support in favour of a Scottish parliament. However, the petition was prone to a number of weakness. Firstly, it did not threaten any type of sanction should the government choose not to comply with home rule demands. It was believed that with such a demonstration of support, government would not be able to ignore the Convention and no planning was made to take account of this eventuality.[24] The Cabinet, however, had recognised that support for home rule would not break traditional political loyalties and that although Scottish national sentiment was powerful, it could be appeased with greater attention within the current Westminster structure. Few ministers expected that home rule would be able to break traditional voting habits and the result of the Paisley by election seemed to confirm this.[25] A second problem with the campaign was that it was not democratically accountable. This weakness was targeted by the Scottish Secretary, Hector McNeill, who challenged the Convention to use the normal party political apparatus to further its claims. If Scottish home rule was so important and popular, it was argued, then the Scottish electorate could vote for Convention candidates.[26] Given that the *raison d'être* of the

Convention was to demonstrate popular support without using the parliamentary process, this was not a realistic option. Finally, doubts were raised as to the authenticity of a number of signitures. The appearance of 'Queen Victoria' and the names of other sundry dead celebrities undermined the seriousness of the endeavour.   The Convention's bluff was called and the campaign evaporated. In any case, the succession of two general elections in 1950 and 1951 soon concentrated the electorate's mind back to conventional party politics.

Although the failure of the Convention was seen a a major set-back for the prospects of a Scottish parliament, its long term effect on the nationalist movement was quite beneficial. Firstly, it removed from the debate the key issue of strategy which had dogged the movement since its inception. The unequivocal failure of the Convention removed pressure group tactics from the nationalist agenda leaving the pursuit of an electoral mandate as the only viable option. The SNP won by default and from now on the party was left as the sole flag bearer of the nationalist movement. This point was reinforced by the fact that many nationalists had dual membership of both the SNP and the Convention and although there was two separate organisation, the incident is best understood from the perspective that this was an internal debate among nationalists. The removal of the Convention option meant that there was no alternative to building up the party as an independent political organisation with all the paraphernalia of a distinctive party. Secondly, it vindicated the hard-liners in the SNP and boosted their credibility among the rank and file. This was essential to resolve the confusion that existed in both the minds of the public and the minds of many nationalists as to the status of a future Scottish parliament. In an endeavour to attract as much support as possible, the issue was always vague so that moderates, devolutionists and separatist could all endorse the objective. The SNP, however, was in favour of independence and, as the only viable nationalist organisation left standing after the debacle of the Convention, nationalists of all types had to accept the party's separatist stance or face the political wilderness. Indeed, Donaldson and McIntyre kept firm to this point to such an extent that several splinter groups did emerge, although all proved to be short lived. Although the division over strategy had weakened the nationalist movement in the late forties and early fifties, its resolution did much to clarify and reinforce the stand taken by the SNP in its constitution and objectives of 1947.

Under the leadership of McIntyre and Donaldson, the SNP began the slow process of building up a credible and distinctive political party. The attractiveness of the Convention approach had been its speed, and this had no doubt seduced many members of the rank and file of the SNP. Yet, there was now no alternative and McIntyre had repeatedly warned members that there would be no quick fix. Instead, the party could only expect hard work and a long, slow haul on the road to independence.[27] The SNP did not do well in by elections or general elections in the fifties. Limited resources meant that the party could not contest more than a handful of seats. The maximum achieved was five in the general election of 1959. Furthermore, given the limited number of seats contested, it was obvious to the electorate that the party was incapable of emerging as a major force in Scottish politics. Yet, experience was gained and organisational skills were improved. Also, the party chose the same seats in each general election which established a growing local presence and although not by any means spectacular, the nationalist share of the vote did steadily improve. The party also made strenuous efforts to recruit new members and disseminate propaganda. Policy was refined and endeavours were made to make the party more distinctive so that something different could be offered from either the Tories or Labour. Robert McIntyre promoted the SNP as a 'middle way' between the capitalist Conservative Party and the socialist Labour Party and the nationalists adopted a social democrat outlook on social and economic policies.

Yet, the critical factor working against the SNP in the fifties was the ideological climate. Nationalism was perceived as romantic and backward looking and, in left wing circles, still suffered a bad press as a result of nationalism during the Second World War.[28] Although the corporate economy had been established during the war, its full implications were only gradually realised. The economic and social objectives of both the main parties were set within the framework of British planning. In 1957, the Labour Party openly rejected Scottish home rule on the grounds that it would economically imperil the nation.[29] The social and economic regeneration of Scottish society required the resources of the British state and for most Scots, it was paying dividends. The British state had provided health care via newly established British institutions. Rising wages and full employment was delivered by the planned economy. Although nationalist sentiment grumbled now and then, much of it was middle-class in origin. Discontent was generated more by symbolic neglect, rather than economic or social grievances. The role of ministers of the Church of Scotland in the Scottish Convention, the middle-class outrage at the use of the numeral II in the Queen's title, the antics of middle-class students in stealing the Stone of Destiny or electing John MacCormick as Rector of Glasgow University, were a world away from the everyday realities of most Scots. The memories of the hungry thirties were still close at hand and when they were contrasted with the prosperity of the affluent fifties, few Scots wanted to change the system of government, no matter how important they regarded or felt Scottish national identity. Being British made economic and social sense and the Union remained unchallenged.

NOTES

[1] P. Addison, *The Road to 1945*, (London, 1975)

[2] R. Saville, 'The Industrial Background to the Post-War Scottish Economy', in R. Saville (ed), *The Economic Development of Modern Scotland*, (Edinburgh, 1980), pp. 1-47.

[3] K. Morgan, *Labour in Power, 1945-51*, (Oxford, 1984).

[4] *ibid.*, A. Cairncross, *Years of Recovery: British Economic Policy, 1945-51*, (London, 1985); H. Pelling, *The Labour Governments, 1945-51*, (London, 1984); P. Thane, *The Foundations of the Welfare State*, (London, 1982); J. Tomlinson, *Employment Policy: The Crucial Years, 1939-55*, (Oxford, 1987).

[5] R. Roger (ed), *Scottish Housing in the Twentieth Century*, (Leicester, 1987)

[6] Scottish Economic Committee, *Scotland's Industrial Future: The Case for Planned Development*, (London, 1939); *A People's Plan for Scotland*, (Glasgow, 1945); John Gollan, *Scottish Prospect: An Economic, Administrative and Social Survey*, (Glasgow, 1948).

[7] See *The Clyde Valley Regional Plan 1946*, (London, 1948).

[8] G. McCrone, *Regional Policy in Britain*, (London, 1970), pp. 106-20.

[9] R. Kelf-Cohen, *British Nationalisation, 1945-73*, (London, 1973).

[10] G. McCrone, *Scotland's Economic Progress, 1951-60*, (London, 1965), pp. 13-20.

[11] Catto (Chairman), *Report on Scottish Financial and Trade Statistics*, Cmnd. 8609 (HMSO, 1952).

[12] *Scotsman*, 24 Oct 1952.

[13] A.D. Campbell, 'Income', in A.K. Cairncross (ed), *The Scottish Economy*, (Cambridge, 1954), pp. 46-65.

[14] P.L. Payne, 'The Decline of the Scottish Heavy Industries, 1945-83', in Saville (ed), *The Economic Development of Modern Scotland*, pp. 79-114.

[15] Statistics taken from the *Scotsman*, 4 Dec. 1952.

[16] *ibid.*

[17] *Scottish Control: Scottish Affairs: Unionist Policy*, (Glasgow, 1949).

[18] *ibid.*, p. 1.

[19] See J. Mitchell, *Conservatives and the Union: A Study of Conservative Party Attitudes to Scotland*, (Edinburgh, 1990), pp. 17-37.

[20] Archie Lamont, *Scotland's Wealth and Poverty*, (Glasgow, 1952).

[21] James Mitchell, 'Scotland and the Union Since 1945' in T.M. Devine & R.J. Finlay (eds), *Scotland in the Twentieth Century*, (Edinburgh, 1996).

[22] *Scottish Control: Scottish Affairs*.

[23] See J. Mitchell, *Strategies for Self-Government: The Campaign for a Scottish Parliament*, (Edinburgh, 1996), pp. 113-36.

[24] NLS, Records of the Scottish Convention.

[25] Mitchell, 'Scotland and the Union'.

[26] *Scotsman*, 30 July 1950.

[27] R.D. McIntyre, *Some Principles of Scottish Reconstruction*, (Glasgow, 1944).

[28] See J.Strachey, *The Balkanisation of Britain*, (London, 1957).

[29] *Glasgow Herald*, 15 June 1957.

CHAPTER SEVEN

The Rise and Fall of the SNP, 1967-79

The period of the mid to late sixties marked a turning point in the fates of both British corporatism and Scottish nationalism. Although with hindsight deep seated structural problems could be detected in the Scottish economy by the late fifties, they were not necessarily apparent to contemporaries who believed that they could be overcome by modifications in the state apparatus and better state planning. By the late sixties, however, the problems of the Scottish economy were even more deeply entrenched and for most Scots the answer to these difficulties was greater government endeavour. It was the failure of the British state to fulfil the socio-economic aspirations of the Scottish people in the late sixties and seventies which provided the stimulus to increasing SNP support. Furthermore, the period also witnessed a transformation in the organisation and internal dynamics of the nationalist movement. This combination of internal and external factors provides the explanation for the growth of the SNP from the late sixties.

The economic history of Scotland in the sixties is a woeful tale of missed opportunities, bad management, poor productivity and under achievement. A central aspect of planning was that the reliance on the traditional heavy industries would be offset by the growth of new consumer industries. A key problem with the traditional industries was that they received neither from public or private sources any form of substantial investment.[1] Production techniques remained backward and labour intensive, design was lamentable and rates of productivity poor.[2] Together with troubled labour relations, bad management and almost non existent marketing, shipbuilding, steel, heavy engineering and coal failed to match the levels of competence achieved either with foreign competitors or sister industries south of the border. It was in response to such concerns that the government commissioned the Toothill report of 1961 which called for more planning and targeted regional assistance.[3] It was believed that job losses in the traditional industries could be offset by attracting new industry north, but this would depend on having a vibrant domestic economy with money to spend on consumer durables. By building up the social infrastructure through a programme of hospital, school, road and public housing construction, full employment could be maintained, social amenities improved and prosperous markets created for new industry. The connection between Scottish economic well-being and British state economic policy was now explicit and would become more explicit as time moved on. The facilitation of such policies required a massive investment in the construction of a state apparatus. As a consequence, the existing arm of government in Scotland, the Scottish Office, expanded from 2,400 civil servants in 1937 to over 8,000 by 1970.[4] The Balfour Report of 1953 recommended that wherever practical, the function of government in Scotland should be handled by the Scottish Office. Indeed, it is interesting to note that while the expansion of the role of the British state in social and economic life necessitated the growth of centralised government, it did not lead to the creation of a uniform government apparatus in the United Kingdom.[5] Rather, this apparatus was grafted on to the existing arms of government in Scotland which had the appearance of creating separate state machinery within a wider state apparatus.[6] All of which led to the creation of a separate and distinctive arm of government in Scotland which enabled the Scottish Secretary to wield even greater powers without direct account to the Scottish electorate. This would return to haunt the Scottish electorate after 1979.

The key to understanding Scottish political behaviour in the sixties is that it was driven by expectations regarding state activity and economic and social well-being. Labour benefited in Scotland as it was the most convincing corporatist party. Harlod Wilson's drive for a modern planned economy forged in the 'white heat of technology' had great appeal and many Scots were allured by the propsect of economic and social transformation. Yet, such planning was more or less handicapped from the outset. Labour's fifteen seat lead in Scotland at the general election of 1964 secured the Labour government's seven seat majority in the House of Commons. Economic planning was subsequently sacrificed on the alter of political expediency, especially after 1967 when the SNP won a by-election from Labour. The Scottish Secretary, William Ross, mercilessly used the danger of a nationalist upsurge to screw more money out of the Cabinet and by the late sixties, government expenditure per head in Scotland was running at twenty per cent above the British average.[7] Bad industrial relations, poor and inexperienced planning and planers, wild optimism, oscillating

levels of public expenditure and short-term political calculations all
combined to produce a catalogue of economic failure.[8] The attainment
of the social objectives of full employment and a prosperous society
were increasingly dependent on high levels of government
expenditure. The more the Scottish economy failed to diversify and
attract new industry and services, the more it relied on government and
the more this determined political behaviour. It was a vicious circle and
one that British politicians found impossible to break. The SNP's
victory in the Hamilton by election of 1967 was fuelled by Scottish
social and economic under-achievement. Unemployment was raising in
Scotland, wages were falling behind the rest of the United Kingdom,
there was devaluation of Sterling and as part of a strategy to curb
inflation and arrest the balance of payments problem, the government
was intent on pursuing a policy of wage restraint.[9] All of which was
grist to the SNP's mill. Labour was rejected at the polls because it was
seen to be failing to deliver and meet the aspirations of the post-war
generation. The SNP was an effective party of protest and an even
more effective way of making British politicians take note.

The SNP's victory in Hamilton did not come from nowhere. The
party had been improving its electoral performance throughout the
sixties. In the general elections of 1964 and 1966 the SNP had put up
fifteen and twenty three candidates and, although relatively
insignificant, its share of the vote had gone up. In the Pollock by
election of March 1967, the party polled twenty eight per cent of the
vote and over 60, 000 votes in Glasgow in the May local elections of
that year. The early sixties also witnessed a dramatic infusion of new
talent into the ranks of the party. Billy Wolfe, Winnie Ewing, Tom
McAlpine, Gordon Wilson, Isobel Lindsay and many others brought to
the party a youthful sense of dynamism coupled with a flair for
organisation and publicity.[10] The youthful vigour of the SNP's
organisation contrasted favourably with the run down Labour machine
which had degenerated into comfortable factions of self-interest, most
of whom could not project beyond the social club or town council.
Nothing breeds success like success and the victory in Hamilton was
followed up by a massive influx of members and in May 1968, the
party won a third of the vote in the local elections. For many, it
appeared as if the Scottish National Party had come of age.[11]

The SNP's success proved to be unsustainable in the short-term.[12] There were signs that the party had peaked by the late sixties and the results in the 1970 general election were disappointing. Its main impact, however, was on the policy development of the Conservative and Labour parties. In 1968 at the party conference in Perth, the Conservative leader, Ted Heath, came out in support of a Scottish assembly. Heath was motivated by a belief that Scottish nationalism would continue to remain a growing political force and that steps had to be taken to counteract it.[13] A salient factor may have been that as a party in opposition, the espousal of devolution would have added to the Labour government's difficulties and wrong footed them, especially when it came to by-elections. The Declaration of Perth, as it was subsequently dubbed, was by no means a carefully formulated policy. Indeed, it was extremely vague and woolly with many key aspects of policy undeveloped and unexplained. Furthermore, Heath imposed the policy on an unwilling Scottish party which had been nurtured on a century's worth of hostility to a Scottish parliament. The policy went against basic Unionist instincts and many party members complained about a lack of consultation and the hierarchy's skin deep knowledge of Scottish affairs. For many it was part of the endeavour to modernise the party which had been one of the key reasons why the name 'Unionist' had been demoted in favour of 'Conservative' in the party's title in 1965. This was not to everybody's liking and paradoxically at the very time when the party was promoting a distinctive Scottish policy, it was saddled with the 'Conservative' label which many complained made the party sound too English.[14] While Heath presented devolution as a major policy innovation, it had the effect of creating confusion and disillusionment among many rank and file Scottish Conservatives. Among the rest the United Kingdom party, it passed by almost unnoticed.

Labour's response was prevarication. The Prime Minister, Harold Wilson, had more important things to worry about and the conventional wisdom was that nationalism was motivated by short-term socio-economic grievances. If such bread and butter problems could be removed, it was argued, then support for the SNP would evaporate. Wilson appointed Lord Crowther to head a Royal Commission on the constitution in 1969. In reality, this move was designed to give the appearance of action, although it was plain from the outset that Wilson was buying time. The Commission was, in Wilson's words, to spend years taking minutes and there was an expectation that when the report finally arrived, the problem would have gone away or it would be left to somebody else to deal with. In any case, the SNP seemed to have been halted shortly after the Commission was initiated. The SNP made only modest gains in the local elections in May 1969 and at the Gorbals by election in October, the party only notched up twenty five per cent of the vote which was widely interpreted as a set back.[15] In the general election of 1970, the nationalists contested sixty five seats which was the largest number to date. Expectations were high as the party's organisation was in good shape and, given the media attention over the last three years, many were confident that there would be a considerable nationalist impact on Scottish electoral politics. This was not to be the case. Although the SNP polled over eleven per cent of the vote, again the best nationalist performance to date, the party lost its seat in Hamilton and only gained the Western Isles. For many, this was enough evidence that the nationalist phenomenon of the late sixties was a short-term, rogue affair; a flash in the pan and of little consequence.[16]

The underlying structural problems in the Scottish economy which generated the nationalist upsurge, however, were not so transient. Ted Heath was elected to power in the United Kingdom with the self-appointed task of rectifying the major defects which had plagued the British economy. Unfortunately, this was wishful thinking and the 'giants' of the British disease, such as the public sector deficit, the negative balance of payments, poor labour relations and the omni-present threat of unemployment, became worse and, in spite of the rhetoric, Heath was forced to spend more public money than any other prime minister to date on appeasing these problems.[17] The failure of corporatism and government planning reached its apogee in November 1973 with the imposition of the three day week which had been caused by the miner's strike and the effects of an oil crisis initiated by the Arab Israeli war. It was in this mood of mounting crisis that Harold Wilson and the Labour Party won the first general election of 1974 in February. The nationalists also emerged as a major force in Scottish politics. As we shall see, however, the rise of the SNP in the mid seventies was the Scottish response to the British crisis.

A number of factors had combined to make the timing of this crisis especially fortuitous for the SNP. The Kilbrandon Commission reported in October 1973 and recommended the setting up of a Scottish assembly. Heath's flirtation with devolution had come to nothing and the publication of the report helped to draw the political focus in Scotland back to constitutional issues.[18] The discovery of north sea oil was likewise, fortuitous. Given that there was an oil crisis, the prospect of an independent Scotland made rich by drawing on its reserves of black gold helped SNP propaganda. The party launched 'It's Scotland's Oil' campaign and comparisons of the future between 'rich Scot' or 'poor Briton' were drawn.[19] Although there is little evidence to suggest that the discovery of oil had any major effect on the voting behaviour of the Scottish electorate, it was important in giving the nationalist movement a significant psychological boost.[20] A perennial problem that party had in mooting the independence option was the fear that Scotland was economically dependent on England. Although claims and counter claims were made about the financial relations between the two countries, the fact that oil was found in Scottish waters seemed to tip the balance and render the notion that Scotland could not survive economically redundant. Again while this may not have impacted upon Scottish society generally, it was, nevertheless, a powerful tool in the SNP's propaganda armoury. Finally, little relief seemed in prospect for the mounting problems of the Scottish economy. Indications that the SNP was on the move came from two by election results in 1973. In March the party polled thirty per cent of the vote in Dundee East and in November, Margo MacDonald won Govan, one of Labour's safest seats.

The general elections of 1974 were the high points of SNP electoral success. In February the party won seven seats which rose to eleven seats in the October election. The nationalists did especially well in former Conservative seats; nine out of the eleven had formerly been held by the Tories. Although Labour put it about that the SNP was doing well because of disaffected Conservatives switching allegiance, the truth of the matter was that the nationalist were the prime beneficiaries of an anti-Conservative bloc in these constituencies.[21]

Labour was only too eager to present the SNP as a right wing movement and play down the fact that former Labour supporters were switching to them. The Conservative constituencies which fell to the SNP were mainly rural seats with little or no Labour presence as the party was notoriously reluctant to build up its rural organisation.[22] The SNP filled the vacuum and was able to solicit support in the towns and housing schemes. Although the SNP attained over thirty per cent of the vote in the second general election, it should not be assumed that all these voters endorsed the party's policy of independence. While it is difficult to accurately assess the real intentions of voters, and here we are very much at the mercy of opinion pollsters whose methods often change and whose findings are subject to disputed readings, it can be confidently assumed that no more than twelve per cent of the electorate agreed with the policy of independence.[23] The SNP was the prime beneficiary of an anti-Conservative vote and it was also an effective option to put pressure on London government to solve a growing sense of Scottish grievance. The fact that the SNP aroused greater interest south of the border than any other configuration of Scottish political behaviour meant that it was a simple and direct method to put Scotland firmly on the British political agenda at a time when it was over crowded with other priorities. Further evidence that the SNP was a party of protest can be found in the social profile of the SNP vote. Again we are very much at the mercy of the political scientists here, but it does seem to be the case that the party was attracting a broad spectrum of Scottish society into its orbit.[24] The fact that the SNP made its appeal in a generalist and non class or interest specific manner reinforced this trend. The party also attracted young voters who are notoriously fickle. The key difficulty facing the SNP was that it had a soft base of support. As an amalgam of interests, it was very difficult to hold a grouping such as this together. Deeper political convictions were not likely to be forthcoming and, as happened in 1979, prone to evaporate.

Although with the benefit of hindsight such difficulties in shoring up the SNP vote become apparent, this was not the picture painted by contemporaries.[25] As the economic crisis deepened, it appeared as if the SNP support would keep on rising. While the Conservatives suddenly re-discovered their devolutionist principals of the late sixties, the Labour government's response was decidedly more ambiguous. The tried and trusted method of buying time was used and it was announced that discussions about the constitution would take place and that proposals would be forthcoming. Yet, Labour was deeply divided over the issue, especially in Scotland. There was an influential faction committed to the principle of British state planning and was exceptionally hostile to Scottish nationalism. The period between the elections in 1974 was dominated by Labour prevarication on the issue of devolution with expediency the key determinant of policy. In April the STUC gave strong support for devolution while the Scottish Executive rejected it in June, only to be overturned in August by a special party conference. Whatever the motivation, it was believed that this ambiguous response had not stopped the SNP which had made further gains in the October general election, including one seat from Labour.

Labour essentially had two options at its disposal for a strategy to combat the growth of Scottish nationalism. One would be to concede political power of some kind to a Scottish parliament. This, it was hoped, would take the steam out of the SNP and satisfy the Scots aspirations for some form of self-government. It would also fit in more neatly with a demand for greater autonomy, which it was believed was the preferred option of most people rather than independence. A second strategy would be to tackle the Scottish grievances at source which was giving rise to Scottish nationalism. A consistent fear in the minds of many anti-devolutionist was that a Scottish parliament which is unable to tackle fundamental economic problems would merely become a focal point for nationalist discontent which would inevitably lead to the break up of the United Kingdom.[26] It should come as no surprise therefore, to find that tried and trusted methods of appeasement were employed first. Promises were made that more industrial powers would be transferred to the Scottish Office in order to beef up the Scottish economy and in July 1975 the Scottish Development Agency was set up. However, it could do little to halt the almost terminal decline of the Scottish economy as mounting unemployment, coupled with deteriorating industrial relations, failed to appease nationalist discontent. Furthermore, as well as the problems of the economy, the Labour government was divided over the issue of

Europe and, to cap it all, nationalist sentiments were emanating from within the Scottish party. A call for a Scottish assembly to have wide ranging economic powers was defeated in March and a compromise was reached in August which would devolve on some form of elected structure the powers held by the Scottish Secretary of State. All in all, it was an extremely difficult time for the Labour government which was dependent on a narrow majority and, after March 1977, was dependent on Liberal support.[27]

In November 1975, the government published its proposals for a devolved Scottish assembly. It would have no revenue raising powers and sovereignty would still be retained in Westminster. Opinion polls conducted over the next six months showed strong support and the breakaway of a Scottish labour party led by Jim Sillars seemed to confirm an unstoppable momentum.[28] Yet, there were a number of factors which would ensure that the passage of devolution legislation would not be a smooth one. The Callaghan government stumbled from one crisis to another. Consequently, given the wide range of competing priorities for government attention ranging from the crisis loan of the International Monetary Fund, the need to court Liberal support for a minority government, public expenditure cuts and industrial unrest, Callaghan and his ministers would be hard pushed to devote much time to the issue. It would have to be fitted in with other competing interests which many in his own party regarded as more important.[29] Labour was badly divided over the issue with leading figures from both camps publicly displaying their hostility to one and other. The government was forced to concede a referendum on the issue in December 1976. As was pointed out at the time, it was the usual government response to a problem which was dividing the party. It was not a convincing display of commitment. Also, given that Labour's *volte face* on the issue of devolution was motivated by the need to halt the rise of the SNP, the nationalist progress was fundamental to determining the government's response and sense of urgency. All eyes turned on the SNP.

Initially the signs were ominous for the government. Labour lost ground in the local election of May 1977 to the SNP which was followed up by the first and second readings of the bill in parliament in November. However, an attempt to impose a guillotine motion on the bill which would limit the amount of parliamentary time devoted to discussion failed. Furthermore, this also opened the way for the imposition of amendments which could substantially alter the government's initial proposals. Given the fractious nature of parliament and the open hostility of many Labour MPs, this was disastrous for the successful implementation of the government's programme. The 'Cunningham amendment' was passed in January 1978 which stipulated that the Bill would not be implemented unless more than forty per cent of the total electorate voted in favour of an assembly. This was topped off with a further amendment that the Orkney's and Shetland islands would be excluded from the scheme if they returned a no vote. Given the centrality of North Sea oil to the future of Scotland's economic prosperity, the implications were clear for all to see. Further tampering came from Tam Dalyell in February when it was stipulated that should parliament be dissolved before the referendum it would not take place until three months after polling day. Not only was the government seen to be less than fully committed and unable to control its parliamentarians, the issue was taking up an inordinate amount of parliamentary time, much to the chagrin of many MPs. Furthermore, the progress of the Bill was testament to the weakness of the Callaghan administration.

By 1978, there were signs that the Scottish economy was starting to pick up and more importantly for the anti-devolutionists, the rise of the SNP seemed to have been stopped. At a number of significant by elections, the nationalists failed to dislodge Labour and in the regional elections, the party failed to make significant gains. While pro-devolutionists in the Labour Party congratulated themselves that the commitment to a Scottish assembly had paid dividends and was diffusing the nationalist threat, anti-devolutionists interpreted the results differently. It was argued that as the issue had come under public scrutiny, the electorate was beginning to take cold feet and that the opinion polls were now showing diminishing support.[30] Both sides took comfort from the halt of the nationalist and the ambiguous nature of the polls led to further confusion. The SNP was left in a cleft stick. On the one hand, many believed that the 'stepping stone' approach to Scottish independence via devolution was viable and that the party ought to support the proposals. Others believed that it was an anti-nationalist device which would impede progress by saddling the Scots with a toothless assembly. Also, it was believed that it would help bale out a floundering Labour government and party. SNP strategy was a compromise, and the nationalists supported the 'Yes' campaign half-heartedly, although it was apparent to all and sundry that few believed in it.[31] The parliamentary SNP fared no better in this atmosphere of confusion. The party had tried to carve out a distinctive niche and political identity for itself. Part of this process involved the cultivation of an even-handed approach to both the Labour government and the Conservative opposition. A problem with this strategy, however, was that the SNP were sandwiched in the middle of mutual Labour and Conservative hostility. The nationalists were attacked as right wing 'tartan Tories' by Labour who pointed out that the SNP did well in Conservative areas; the implication being that the party support was dependent on former Tory voters. The Conservatives, for good measure, accused the nationalists of being socialist and raised the spectre of an independent Scotland which was dominated by the left wing central belt.[32] SNP support, as we have seen, in the former Conservative seats was based on an anti-Tory coalition of interests which tended to be more working-class in its composition. The even handed approach of the parliamentary SNP, far from carving out a distinctive political identity, simply added to the confusion. Furthermore, when coupled with the ambiguous approach of the party to the devolution campaign, it simply convinced many that it was a movement of 'ditherers'.[33]

If anything, the devolution debate of the late seventies showed the extent to which the Scots were divided over the issue. The 'Yes' campaign was weakened by ambivalent SNP support, divided Labour loyalties, inadequate finance and poor organisation. The 'No' campaign, on the other hand, was supported by business, well funded, thoroughly organised and did not have any muddy lines of ambiguity which plagued the 'Yes' camp. Public debate on the issue further exposed many of weakness associated with the issue. For some, the whole question of the Scots running themselves was preposterous. Historians were wheeled out to show that the Scots had always been incapable of governing themselves in the past.[34] Some argued that Scottish society would degenerate into the chaos of religious sectarianism reminiscent of Northern Ireland.[35]　　Others made great play of the sentimental attachment to England and Britain which should not be thrown over in a moment of weakness.[36] Although the vote in March 1979 showed a majority of those who voted in favour; 51.6 said yes, 48.4 said no, it was hardly a ringing endorsement. Almost forty per cent did not bother to vote. While a syndrome of 'we were robbed' has grown up about the devolution referendum, the truth of the matter is that it, more than anything, showed how ambivalent the Scots were to the issue. While a plethora of interpretations have sprung up to account for the failure of the referendum, ranging from the idea that devolution was associated in the electorate's mind with a dying and unpopular government to a national psychosis resulting from he defeat of Ally's tartan army in Argentina,　the fact remains that the rise of the SNP was the Scottish electorate's response to a British crisis.

As was mentioned earlier, the opinion poll evidence showed that of those voting for the SNP, a majority did not agree with the party's key policy of independence. All of which suggests tactical voting.[37] Furthermore, there is a strong correlation between the SNP vote and economic performance. Crudely put, when the Scottish economy appeared to be doing well, people were less likely to vote nationalist. The SNP was an effective way of putting pressure on British government to take Scottish problems seriously. What the Scottish electorate appeared to want was more corporatism, more government intervention in the economy and more public expenditure. The SNP was only a means to achieve this, as it was quite clear that the objectives of the Scottish National Party were incompatible with these goals. The Scots, as was argued earlier, were fully embedded into the values and aspirations of the post-war consensus politics. As London government found it increasingly more and more difficult to meet the aspirations of the Scottish electorate, the more pronounced was the tendency to turn to nationalism, but only as a means to make or coerce British politicians deliver the goods.　The fiasco of the devolution referendum in 1979 had called the Scottish electorate's bluff and in the 1979 general election the Scottish card was not played. The SNP lost over a third of its support as it deserted back to Labour as the best bet to fulfil the corporatist dream.

One final myth must be laid to rest before concluding this chapter. It has become an established part of Labour folk lore that it was the SNP which heralded the advent of Thatcherism. After the referendum defeat the SNP tabled a vote of no confidence in the Commons resulting in the fall of Callaghan's government and the general election of 1979 which the Conservative Party won. In the words of the former prime minister, the turkeys voted for an early Christmas as the SNP lost nine of its eleven seats.[38] Yet, in many ways the nationalists had no option. With devolution dead, the party's credibility was severely dented. One of the key reasons for voting for the SNP was the pressure it could bring to bear on the British political establishment and with the Labour government having clearly failed to deliver, the nationalists believed that there was no other option but to vote no confidence. To have done nothing would have been a very public declaration of impotence. Obviously, the results of the 1979 general election show that, to some extent, the SNP was punished for bringing done the government. Yet, to attribute the Conservative victory to the SNP is nonsense. The Conservatives won the general election because of Labour's unpopularity in Britain as a whole and because the Conservative Party fared best in the British electoral system. With the advent of Thatcherism the ideals of the corporatist state came to an end and so did the Scottish post-war dream of a new Britain.

NOTES

[1] See P.L. Payne, ' The Decline of the Scottish Heavy Industries, 1945-83', in R. Saville (ed), *The Economic Development of Modern Scotland, 1950-1980*, (Edinburgh, 1985), pp. 79-114.
[2] Chris Harvie, *No Gods and Precious Few Heroes, 1914-1980*, (London, 1981), pp. 35-64.
[3] J.N. Toothill, *Report on the Scottish Economy*, (Edinburgh, 1960).

[4] I.G.C. Hutchison, 'Government in Scotland', in T.M. Devine and R.J. Finlay (eds), *Scotland in the Twenthieth Century*, (Edinburgh, 1996), pp. 46-64.

[5] See J. Kellas, *The Scottish Political System*, (Cambridge, various editions); M. Keating, A. Midwinter & J. Mitchell, *Politics and Public Policy in Scotland*, (London, 1992).

[6] L. Paterson, *The Autonomy of Modern Scotland*, (Edinburgh, 1995).

[7] Gavin McCrone, 'The Role of Government', in Saville (ed), *Economic Development of Modern Scotland*, pp. 195-214.

[8] Harvie, *No Gods and Precious few Heroes*, pp. 142-45.

[9] McCrone, 'The Role of Government'.

[10] See Billy Wolfe, *Scotland Lives*, (Edinburgh, 1973); J. Brand, *The National Movement in Scotland*, (London, 1979).

[11] See J.N. Wolfe, *Government and Nationalism in Scotland*, (Edinburgh, 1969) for a contemporary assessment of nationalism's prospects in Scotland.

[12] See W. Miller, *The End of British Politics*, (Oxford, 1981).

[13] J. Mitchell, 'Scotland and the Union Since 1945' in devine and Finlay (eds), *Scotland in the Twentieth Century*, p. 95.

[14] J. Mitchell, *Conservatives and the Union: A Study of Conservative party Attitudes to Scotland*, (Edinburgh, 1990), p. 56.

[15] *Scotsman*, 19 June 1970.

[16] See I. MacLean, 'The Rise and Fall of the Scottish National Party', *Political Studies*, 18 (1970) for a contemporary assessment.

[17] S. Ball & A. Seldon (eds), *The Heath Government: A Reappraisal*, (London, 1996).

[18] *See Scotsman*, 4 Nov. 1973.

[19] *ibid.*, 12 March 1973.

[20] See W. Miller, 'The Connection Between SNP Voting and the Demand for Self-Government', *European Journal of Political Research*, 5 (1978).

[21] See Miller, *The End of British Politics*.

[22] Harvie, *No Gods and Precious Few Heroes*, p. 148.

[23] Miller, "The Connection Between SNP Voting'.

[24] See D. McCrone, 'We're a' Jock Thamson's Bairns: Social Class in Twentieth Century Scotland', in Devine and Finlay (eds), *Scotland in the Twentieth Century*, pp. 119.

[25] See *Scotsman* 1 Nov. 1975.

[26] T. Dalyell, *Devolution: The End of Britain*, (London, 1977).

[27] See A. Thorpe, *A History of the British Labour Party*, (London, 1997).

[28] H. Drucker, *Breakaway: The Scottish Labour Party*, (Edinburgh, 1978).

[29] See William Rodgers, 'Government Under Stress: Britain's Winter of Discontent', *Political Quarterly*, 55 (1984).

[30] See J. Mitchell, *Strategies for Self-Government: The Campaign for a Scottish Parliament*, (Edinburgh, 1996), pp. 204-21.

[31] *Ibid.*

[32] *Ibid.*

[33] *Ibid.*

[34] See Neil MacCormick (ed), *The Scottish Debate*, (Oxford, 1970).

[35] *Glasgow Herald*, 8 Aug 1978.

[36] See Chris Harvie, *Scotland and Nationalism:Scottish Society and Politics, 1707-1977*, (London, 1977 edn), pp. 283-87.

[37] Miller, *The End of British Politics*.

[38] D. Butler, *The General Election of 1979*, (London, 1980).

CONCLUSION
Doomsday and After, 1979-97

The campaign for a Scottish parliament became one of the most important facets of Scottish politics in the eighties. Opinion polls conducted throughout this decade invariably showed that between seven and eight out of every ten Scots wanted some form of constitutional change. The defenders of the *status quo* were a small minority. Such attitudes were reflected in political developments. As the only party opposed to any form of constitutional realignment, the Conservative Party in Scotland has seen its support plummet to unthinkable depths. From winning over fifty per cent of the popular vote in the general election in 1955, the party in 1997 had no MPs and a derisory seventeen per cent of the vote. Nor was this totally unexpected. Scottish political history after 1979 is mainly a sorry tale of every declining Conservative popularity.[1] Yet, it would be wrong to claim that the demand for some form of Scottish parliament was the principal catalyst of political change north of the border. Rather, the demand for constitutional change, of whatever shape or form, has been motivated by the changed political realities the Scots faced after 1979.

Although few expected it, the advent of the Thatcher regime in the eighties irrevocably changed Scottish political behaviour and perceptions of the British state. It did this in two ways. Firstly, it set in train anti-Conservative voting behaviour. Secondly, it forced many Scots to reassess the power of the British state apparatus in Scottish society.

It has been the decline of the Conservatives which has marked the political divergence of Scotland and England in the period since 1979. Although the Labour Party has emerged as the strongest political party north of the border, much of this is due to tactical anti-Conservative voting. The following reasons may be suggested for the decline of Tory Party fortunes north of the border. Firstly, the attack on corporatism was not widely endorsed by the Scottish middle-class. Indeed, to some extent, corporatism had become part and parcel of Scottish middle-class values as many had benefited substantially form these policies in the past. Generations of upwardly mobile Scots had received a good comprehensive education and had gone to university courtesy of the Welfare State. The employment profile of Scotland also suggests that a great many middle-class Scots earn their living in the public sector. The values of the Welfare State and comprehensive education were more firmly entrenched in the political culture of the Scots. Paradoxically, just as Scotland and England were becoming more similar in terms of social profile, the gap in political behaviour widened.[2] The Conservative attack on corporatism and the 'nanny state' was perceived as an attack on Scottish political culture *per se*. The traumatic experience of de-industrialisation and the collapse of traditional heavy industry further damaged Conservative popularity. Secondly, the Conservatives were unable to promote a distinctive Scottish policy and the party was increasingly seen as the party of middle England, upon which the Conservative electoral hegemony rested. The imposition of unpopular legislation, such as the poll tax and school boards, were regarded as southern English inventions. The vacuum in Unionist ideology which had been plugged with corporatism reappeared and exposed significant contradictions in Conservative philosophy. In England the message was independence and self reliance; the state would take a back seat. In Scotland it was a return to the message of the thirties that the Scots were subsidised and dependent on government expenditure. As the opposition parties put some form of self-government at the centre of their Scottish policies the Tories increasingly used the argument of dependency in defence of the Union. Apart from saying different things in Scotland and England, the dependency argument is not one that readily appeals to the traditional middle-class voter. Unionism was negative and defeatist and in spite of the *Taking Stock* exercise which attempted to promote Scotland as a nation within the Union (the decision to host the European Summit in Edinburgh as a European capital in 1993 is a good example of the attempt to regenerate Scottish nationality within the Union), the Conservatives in Scotland lacked the vital Scottish dimension which the opposition parties had. The third and final reason why Conservative support has plummeted concerns British identity in Scotland. Corporatism and the Welfare State were instrumental in making the Scots feel that the Union with Britain was working. The Welfare State and the managed economy were vital in promoting a new sense of Britishness in Scotland after 1945 and by and large this held good until 1979. However, the Thatcherite attack on consensus values robbed the

Scots of an acceptable vision of Britain and paradoxically, the upsurge in Scottish nationalism has been fuelled by a desire to preserve what are fundamentally British institutions such as the health service and comprehensive education. The Scots have painted the ideology of welfare statism tartan and called it their own.[3] The point to be stressed is that in fundamentals, the English nation changed its political values in 1979 more so than the Scots and as such Conservatism and the Conservative governments have been interpreted as *English* and alien. It is this cultural perception, more than anything, which explains recent Scottish political behaviour and the decline of Conservatism.

The Labour Party has been the prime beneficiary of the decline in Conservative fortunes. The use of tactical voting to punish Mrs Thatcher resulted in large numbers of Labour MPs being returned in the elections of 1983, 87 and 92. However, Labour's share of the popular vote has not increased correspondingly with its parliamentary representation. While many complained about the British electoral system and its ability to return a large Conservative majority with just over forty per cent of the vote, few voices were raised in protest at the even greater representation the Labour Party secured north of the border. The eighties were a turbulent time for the Labour Party and this was especially the case in Scotland. Whereas the English party veered to the left and in so doing made itself unelectable, the Scottish party remained moderate and maintained its level of support. The problem that the Labour Party in Scotland faced was that its English partner let the side down. For many, it seemed that Labour would never attain power. Furthermore, the policies of the Conservative governments were deeply unpopular and many argued that given the collapse of Tory support, such actions were an imposition against the wishes of the Scottish people. Time and time again, it was reiterated that the Conservative Party did not have a mandate north of the border. As many commentators were aware, Thatcherism fuelled a revival of Scottish nationalism.

It was in response to the activities of the Conservative governments and the sense of Labour's electoral impotence that home rule re-emerged as a serious policy option in Labour circles. Home rule could be used to circumvent the potential nationalist upsurge which was threatening to emerge in response to the imposition of unpopular

Conservative policies and Labour's inability to stop them. A Scottish parliament could act as an anti-Conservative bulwark and defend the Scottish people against the onslaught of an insensitive government which was elected on the basis of southern English votes. A devolved Scottish parliament working within the confines of the British state would also, it was argued, stop the drift towards separation and diffuse the nationalist threat. It was with such objectives in mind that Labour, the Liberal Democrats (who also did well in parliamentary representation as a result of anti-Conservative voting behaviour), the churches, the STUC and local government authorities set to work in the Scottish Constitutional Convention to produce plans for Scottish home rule.[4]

While support for a Scottish parliament was motivated to a large extent by simple political expediency; the need to stop the drift to nationalism and present some form of defence mechanism against an entrenched Tory government, other factors relating to the shape of government in Scotland became important. The 'Democratic Deficit' was the term used to describe the operation of government in Scotland in which the Scots had no democratic input. The deficit was not new and it had not been created in the eighties; it simply became more apparent. The construction of a centrally controlled state apparatus had been a feature of both Conservative and Labour governments in the post-war era. This was not a problem as Scottish political behaviour broadly moved in line with British political behaviour and the actions of central government in Scotland were rarely out of kilter with what the people wanted. The advent of Thatcherism and the use of the state apparatus to drive through unpopular legislation dramatically exposed the democratic deficit and highlighted the lack of accountability of the Scottish Secretary of State and the Scottish Office to the Scottish people. It is to redress this imbalance that home rule has been mooted.

The election of a landslide Labour government in 1997 committed to the creation of a Scottish parliament will mark another chapter in the history of Scottish politics and the Union. Yet, as we have seen, in spite of the best efforts of many committed and enthusiastic individuals, the parliament in Edinburgh is, historically speaking, a most elusive creature. It will take a great deal of political will to succeed in the future where others have failed in the past.

NOTES

[1] See R.J. Finlay, 'Scottish Conservatism and Unionism Since 1918' in M. Francis and I. Zweiniger-Bargielowska (eds), *The Conservatives and British Society, 1880-1990*, (Cardiff, 1996).

[2] David McCrone, 'We're a' Jock Thomson's Bairns: Social Class in 20th Century Scotland' in T.M. Devine and R.J. Finlay (eds), *Scotland in the Twentieth Century*, (Edinburgh, 1996).

[3] For a recent treatment of these themes see David McCrone, *Understanding Scotland: the Sociology of a Stateless Nation* (1992).

[4] Owen Dudley Edwards, *A Claim of Right*, (Edinburgh, 1992).

Index